AF454179

Quramo™

Chiziterem Chijioke is the winner of the Quramo Writers' Prize (2023) for her title, Dear Zimi.

The Quramo Writers' Prize started in 2017 with the sole purpose of discovering unpublished, new strong African voices and showcasing them to the world.

Every year, a new winner is unveiled at the
Quramo Festival of Words (QFest).

Visit our website: www.quramo.com

For more information on the
Quramo Writers' Prize and Quramo Festival.

DEAR ZIMI

ISBN: 978-3-9011-7677-7

Published in Nigeria in 2024 by Quramo Publishing under its QBooks imprint

The Simi Johnson Centre
13 Sinari Daranijo Street, Victoria Island
Lagos, Nigeria.
+234 704 787 2000
info@quramo.com
www.quramo.com

A catalogue record of this book will be available from the National Library of Nigeria.

DEAR ZIMI

CHIZITEREM CHIJIOKE

For my parents:

You believed I could fly, so I soared.

Table of Contents

1

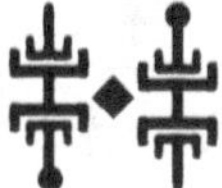

A hollow gnaws at my soul seeking to devour me and I feel as though, at any moment, my entire body would rip to shreds. I board a bus and do not argue with the conductor when he overcharges the fare. I must see Belema. She is the only person who can help me understand this madness and keep the hollowness from consuming me.

Today, Belema's neighbourhood is tranquil. There are no bikes in front of the mosque at the beginning of the street. Ochuko, who lives on Belema's street, does not stand on the veranda to hail me, one hand fanning himself with his shirt as he often did. Tayo, the little girl who lives in the house next to Belema's, does not run towards me to wrap her tiny arms around my knee, letting go only after I have given her a treat or money to get a treat. I am grateful I do not have to talk to anyone. The earth in front of Belema's house is wet. I leap over the algae and sidestep the thicker parts of the mud. When I enter through Belema's gate, my soles are muddy. I drag and stomp my feet on the pavement before entering the house.

I am startled by the heat inside. How has none of the cool breeze blown into the house? Belema stands in the living room in baggy jeans and a batik crop top. She stands before the full-size mirror by the entrance door, her phone in one hand, her other hand placed on her breast. Her red braids, so long they reach her bum, swing with every movement she makes. I stand by the door, rubbing my palms against my teal dress as I tend to do when they are sweaty—and they have been sweaty all morning.

While Belema ignores me and continues to take pictures of herself, I try to stay calm by letting my eyes wander across the living room. The black couch revamped a year ago after Belema's father had sent money for new furniture; the wooden side stools that have been there for as long as I can remember; the framed image of marijuana that was hung on the dirty yellow wall a few months ago after Belema had attested that her most creative moments were associated with weed. My gaze wanders back to Belema still taking pictures. She likes to take about a hundred and then selects one worthy of posting online.

"When did you make this blouse?" I ask, trying to distract myself from the panic I am feeling.

She strikes another pose, her hand now covering her eyes, her tiny lips puckered. She takes a picture, then sighs. "Yesterday, Petite. Is that how you greet?"

"I have been standing here and you've ignored me since," I say. I rub my hands against my dress again, my heart thudding.

Belema groans and turns to me. "You did not tell me you were coming. You should have called."

"Something serious has happened, Belema."

She frowns. "Did you tell your dad about the results? I told you to chill until school resumes before you conclude that the results are without any mistake." She starts walking towards me. "We would meet Dr Lawanson and try to talk to him about it. I am sure he'd allow us to see the records."

"Not everything is about school," I retort. I realise now that I do not know what it is that Belema can supposedly do for me. I do not know if she is even the right person I should first run to with this.

"Zimife!" Belema yells.

"What?" I yell back, startled out of my thoughts. My eyes dampen. I take a step back. I am now leaning against the door frame. My chest is hot, burning as if set ablaze.

"What's wrong, guy?" She asks. Though she is only frowning slightly, it still distorts her face like a physical defect. Always laughing or smiling, frowning has never suited Belema's round face and light skin.

I try to speak but my voice breaks. Tears begin to fall over my cheeks, and I feel my throat closing up.

"Wetin happen?" Belema asks, still frowning.

"Belema," I croak. I see her walk towards me in my blurred vision. I feel her hand on my shoulder. She guides me into the living room and pulls me down gently to sit on the couch.

She fetches a pink handkerchief from her pocket and hands it to me. It smells of weed, but I take it and press it against my eyes.

"Belema, I'm pregnant," I say, my voice breaking. More tears fall and my chest begins to heave.

"You say?" She says and jolts away from me.

I stare at the floor. I see the dust that has accumulated on the black tiles. I move my feet slightly and the dust scatters. Belema is usually lazy about cleaning and living alone makes it worse.

"How did this happen, Petite?" she asks, drawing closer to me. She lifts my face to meet her gaze.

"I don't know," I say in my broken voice. I cry more and rub my hand against my dress. "It just happened."

"No condom?"

I sigh, wiping my face furiously. "It broke."

"Ha," Belema exclaims, her mouth ajar. Her reactions terrify me even more, so I continue to cry. "Why did you not take a postpill?"

"I did not think it entered." I cry.

"But we talk about these things, Zim. How could you be this careless, ehn? Wetin sup na?"

I shake my head and cry. I had thought that I was protected for the most part. I did not think there was going to be any trouble.

"How did you find out?"

"I had been having PMS signs, but my period did not come. Then I vomited two days ago. Plus—a lot of things sha. Then I got scared and decided to take a test." I caught my breath after speaking so fast.

I start to think of my father. He may never look at me the same way again if he finds out about this. He may withdraw all his adoration that made me feel like his favourite. My mother will be furious and embarrassed that one of her daughters got pregnant out of wedlock. The shame it would bring her before her extended family and the catholic women's guild at Ajah where she is held in high esteem. Her elder brother will finally have something to gloat at while he restates why she should not have married my father in the first place. And then there is Nelson. I feel a shiver as I think of him. He would breathe fire down my neck, cut me off and deny that we share the same blood. If I could rid myself of this pregnancy as soon as possible, then all would be well. The earlier I can do that, the better.

Belema looks away and licks her lips. She places a hand on her belly and taps gently. Perhaps this is why my first thought was to come to her. Belema would think with me, cry with me, and proffer a solution; and her ideas always work out. But this is beyond me trying to make my Ds and Cs into As and Bs. It is beyond me struggling to get into a second-class upper. Belema cannot help me here. I begin to cry again.

When I first met Belema, she was screaming out the lyrics of Kizz Daniel's *Madu* while she sketched a dress design on an A4 paper. The room smelled of weed and air freshener, as if she had smoked and then sprayed the room right after to get rid of the smell of weed. Pieces of fabric were littered on the blue rug; the mattress was on the floor and the bunk was broken. When she looked at me, her eyes were red. I decided I would hate her. I was not academically enthusiastic and did not need a roommate that would worsen this. I had hoped for a roommate who would study late into the night and as such encourage me to study as well. Not one who got high right in the middle of a regular day.

I was wrong.

In ways I would come to appreciate, she was the roommate I needed. Belema was Belema and still is. Classes had started when I resumed and, being coursemates, she helped me settle quickly into school work and introduced me to the lecturers and some of our other coursemates. Since Belema studies only during library hours, she would drag me along. Her memory, eidetic, helped us through many tests and examinations.

I was excited when I discovered that our houses in Lagos were not very far from each other. I lived in a small estate at Sangotedo while she lived at Ajiran, inside Agungi—a hood I did not know existed in a place like Lekki. The houses are not duplexes, the roads are not tarred, and electricity is not constant, but the people form a beautiful community that is a reminder of the roots scraped over to build Lagos's Island for the affluent.

Belema's mother died in a road accident when she was ten. With finances tight, her father moved to Jerusalem when she turned fifteen, hoping to get a good job and in turn send money home to his daughter. Before leaving, he placed her under the care of her grandmother, who passed away two years ago.

"But wait o, Zim," Belema said suddenly, "when did you sleep with that man and you did not tell me? Why did you sleep with him?" She is glaring at me now. My hand freezes against my dress.

"What man?" I ask, not looking up at her.

"What do you mean, 'What man?' That Urhobo guy na. The Corper. Abi, is he not the baby daddy?"

I look up now, feeling calmer. "Yes, he is. It happened on Valentine's Day." I say, watching Belema scrunch up her face.

"How come you slept with him? I thought you said you were not certain about your feelings. Abi ear dey pain me?"

I shrug. "It just happened."

"He likes you sha. That guy like you well well, Zimi. But you no really like am and you sleep with am. You used him."

"What?" I glare at her. "Used, how? The sex was consensual, abeg."

"But you are not certain of your feelings for him."

I swallow. "That's not how I see it."

"You have to be careful of how you make these decisions, Petite," she says. I shake my head.

"How has this turned into a pity party for Tobore, abeg? I am the one who is pregnant."

"I am just saying, no dey play with person emotions anyhow. Try dey reason things. You know he likes you. What do you think the sex means for him, for both of you?"

I groan. "I don't even know."

"Well, first you have to tell him about this pregnancy."

"No. I don't want to tell him. He doesn't need to know anything about this for now."

Belema stares at me. "Petite, this thing no be joke o. You are fucking pregnant."

My eyes water again. I pull my head back to keep the tears from falling.

"I fucking know," I say.

"Then what's the plan? What do we do about this?" "I'll abort it," I say pointedly.

Belema cocks her head and stares at me, her face slightly red from all the shouting. She shakes her head.

"Tell the guy first," she says.

"I can't," I whisper. "Fuck!" I yell. I start to cry again.

"I know this is hard, but he deserves to know. I thought you said you guys have been talking and it may lead somewhere. If eventually you guys become serious nko? What will now happen?" I am not certain Tobore and I will become serious. My feelings towards him change every day. We had sex during Valentine's because I was drunk and upset. Although I do not particularly regret it, if I had been sober, we might not have gone through with it.

Tobore and I have been stuck in the talking stage for five months. We met in November when I had gone to a local government centre to get my Permanent Voter's Card. He was one of the corps members coordinating the queue outside before we were ushered in for registration. I had been waiting in line when there was a push, which led a large woman to shove me out of the line and caused me to stagger until I fell butt-flat onto the tarmac. Tobore rushed towards me showing great concern that I might be hurt. Up close, I found him to be good-looking but not staggeringly so. He was tall, with bold facial structures—plump lips, doeeyed and a slightly crooked nose. His confidence made his aura attractive. We began to talk afterwards. He asked for my phone number and I gave it to him.

The more we spoke, the more of him I saw. I felt his tenderness. I feel it when he stares at me. I feel it in how he tries to cosset me with food, how he randomly rubs my leg when my body gives him the go-ahead. I see it when he offers to pay for a ride to take me home rather than take the bus. I feel it when he tries to recommend books to me that could help me grow my business. I feel it in the way he keeps checking up on me, even when I do not respond to his texts for days. I feel it with the YouTube links about optimism and the human mind he sends whenever I am anxious or nervous. I feel it in how he captions the links *I hope this helps you feel better*.

Yet, sometimes, I wonder what he sees in me and why he keeps coming back. Belema says I am cute and that my skin, a deep brown, looks like God dipped it in honey.

"You are an attractive one, Petite. Bank on that," she would say.

I don't see myself as attractive, but sometimes I like to agree that my small figure makes me seem cute. My short height, slender curves, cropped ginger-dyed hair. Tobore said he calls me Sissy because my cuteness has Lagos girl vibes sprinkled over it.

He calls me Sissy such that it sounds like Cee Cee instead of Sisi. Whenever I tried to correct him, he would disagree.

"You are a Sissy, not a Sisi," he had said. And the name stuck.

"Zim," Belema calls. I look at her. She gives me a knowing look.

"What are we doing about this?"

"I told you already: an abortion. I just need to find a way to gather money. Everything I have now is locked in savings till next year." I stand up and run a hand through my cropped hair. I did not comb it before leaving home. I imagine it looks spiky and unkempt now. I hate that.

"If that is what you decide, there is no going back. Guy—" Belema says, looking worried, her pupils larger than they usually are, "Think am well. Abortion or make you kuku tell your folks," she says. I shake my head vigorously.

"You know I've been saying it for the longest time, even as a joke, say if I carry belle, I go commot am."

"I know," Belema says. She moves towards me. "But this is a reality now. Abortion might be safe, or not. We don't know. I know you are scared right now. I am too. What if we don't get enough money to go through with this? Only two of us cannot do what is involved with this, guy."

"So, what are you now saying?" I ask, frowning.

"That we need to involve more people. You wan run abortion, where the money?" She asks, her palms splayed open, her eyes widened. "You need a solid 100k to be certain you can do it. Maybe we both could have come up with the money at a different time, but I started saving my income and you just restarted *Glam Girl*."

My chin drops to my chest. If I had been consistent with my business in the past year, maybe I would be able to immediately find the money for an abortion. I only became serious about the hair business a month ago after the university academic staff union declared a nationwide strike. I took social media content creation seriously and found a means to grow my business.

I feel myself deflating and it is as though only a bit of my soul is left. My heart thuds. I see my mother slap me across my face; my father shakes his head and snaps his fingers in the air; my brother's glare burns through me. I start to cry again.

I do not know where I can get the money from, but I will get it. For now, I need to find a competent abortion clinic in this Lagos.

I do not intend to lose my womb.

2

When the birds begin to chirp, my eyes are already scarlet from tears. The blue curtains are drawn open and the room reveals itself in the unfolding light, its messiness stark. Sobenne, whom I share the room with, has left for work. The room is littered with her clothes—dirty ones as well as the ones she had considered wearing before settling on what she wore to work. The shoe rack against the wall has fallen and the shoes are scattered around it. The wardrobes are open. Thankfully, the clothes inside them are still well-folded and stacked. The corner of the room dedicated to my business is a mess. The large ring light has been pushed too close to the wall so that Sobenne's large box sits before it. The black chair I shoot videos with is covered with clothes. The white wall is so dull that the *Glam Girl* inscribed on it with yellow paint is inconspicuous from where my bed is. The bedside table is littered with biscuit wrappers and a half-filled sachet of water.

For most of my life, I have cleaned up after Sobenne and I am offended that she always expects me to do so. What was so difficult about cleaning up after oneself that she could not do so? If she tried to pick out her outfit a day earlier, her life would be easier. Although she never demands that I clean up after her, I feel obliged because she has seven years on me.

Nonetheless, she is the sibling to whom I feel closest. I feel as close to her as I feel distant from Nelson. Sobenne and I have shared almost everything for as long as I can remember. We started sharing a room because I disliked sleeping alone, especially in the dark. When we had just moved into this house, I had a room to myself and cried most nights. Sobenne could not bear it, so she moved into my room and hers gradually turned into a store for things either of us no longer used but was not willing to throw out. Sobenne is my favourite in the house, after Daddy. She has called me Baby since the day I was born because she had been so excited that she could have a baby to carry, hold, feed, and cradle.

Nelson, on the other hand, behaves as though he is pissed off that our mother birthed me when he was ten. No day goes by that he does not remind me that he is financially responsible for me. I imagine him gloating to himself about being able to do this while our parents are still alive.

I am standing beside the window gazing at the birds perched on the large tree in our neighbour's compound. I like to listen to them chirping and wonder what they are saying to one another. A knock on my door startles me.

"Zimife, I should come and drag you out of the room this morning for prayers. Shouldn't I?" Mummy says in her high-pitched voice; her tone, ever so light. Sometimes, she sounds so English for someone who grew up in Onitsha.

"Shit," I mumble to myself, fleeing from the window. If she catches me still in bed, I would not hear the end of it.

"Zimife?" She calls again.

"Mummy! Good morning!" I call out, trying to hide the crack in my voice. I am afraid that if she sees me now as I am she would know straightaway that I am pregnant. Mummy had known early that Rose, our help many years ago, was pregnant. She had just stared at Rose and said she looked watery, like one whose insides were changing. Mummy had been right. Rose had been six weeks gone and had been drinking lime and Seven Up because she had heard this could induce an abortion.

"I don't know what is good about this morning. Open this door." She pushes the door and the hinges shake, as do my hands pushing back against the door.

"Mummy, I'm a mess right now. I'm naked and looking for what to wear." I dash off to pull out clothes from my wardrobe. I toss my tank top over my head and throw it on the bed, then I pull off my yellow silk trousers. I take the half sachet of water from the nightstand and pour it on my face. I grab Sobenne's towel from the black chair and place it over my shoulder, so it falls over my body.

"Open—" I pull the door open before she can say more, then make a show of shielding my body from her. She is dressed in a knee-length floral dress and white pumps. I wonder why I had not heard her pumps clump as she approached my door. Her makeup stands out—the bloody red lips and the thin line across her shaved eyebrows. Frowning, she looks like an angry Sobenne. They share the same shade of light skin, the same heart-shaped face, large lips, large eyes and even physique—a thick build highlighted by pronounced curves. Sometimes, when I look at mummy, it is like looking at an older Sobenne. I wonder if Daddy had known they would share such a resemblance before naming my elder sister Sobenne, which means *follow after your mother*. When Nelson had asked some years ago, Daddy had said it was a mere coincidence.

"I named her Sobenne because your mother was doing so well in her career. It was the year she completed her master's and everything was going great. I just wanted a name that prayed that she would be like her mother."

Mummy stares at me now with disapproval. Her eyeballs are bouncing about as though she is trying to unravel a mystery.

"Lekwa... Can you imagine? You really are naked. At this time? Your father is shouting that we have not had morning prayers." I open my mouth to speak but I have no excuse.

"Come downstairs now, let us pray before I leave for work. My teachers are looking for me and your father is ravenous," she says and walks away.

"I'll be right there," I say as I shut the door and lean against it.

I sigh. I move away to dress up and go downstairs.

In my family, the year each child was born marks a milestone. The year I was born, Mummy quit her job at a government-owned secondary school in Sagamu to establish her school in Lagos. She had been pregnant with me while running around to get the school started. It was also the year my father's eldest sister, Aunty Theresa—who had put my father through school and had stood in as his parent when my grandmother ran mad after birthing him— died. She had raised him until he came to Lagos to apprentice as a *boi-boi*; and when, to avoid paying my father as was the norm, his Oga had accused him of stealing a large sum, it was Aunty Theresa who had given my father the money to start his own business in Lagos Island. So, when he heard she had collapsed and was admitted to the hospital, he had taken the first bus to Enugu.

Everyone said Aunty Theresa waited to see Daddy before she died. Daddy said she had promised him that she would come again, that she would send him the light that would brighten his life. Two weeks later, Mummy was pregnant. Mummy told me that when my father first held me, he smiled and said, "Look at her, the light Theresa has sent me." And it was then that she knew my name.

Ozimife. *She sent me the light.*

Mummy leaves for work after the morning prayer and I prepare abacha for daddy. He sits in the living room leaning his chin on his knuckles and elbow on the couch's armrest, veins bulging on his wrinkled dark arm. He stares at the wall and the scar above his left eye makes him look mean. I place the meal before him.

"Daddy," I call at him. He flinches, turns to me and smiles. He has the most beautiful smile—he bares his teeth and his dimples sink into his cheeks. I wish I inherited his smile. It is often said that Nelson and I look like our grandfather. The only thing I inherited from Daddy is his dark skin. Daddy always smiles at me as if, with me, he has won a prize. He does not hide that I am his favourite.

"Zim of Africa!" He hails. Although my heart is thudding, I smile. He looks at the meal and nods.

"Thank you, my dear." He picks up the fork. "So, when will they call off this strike? You have stayed at home for too long. By the time they call off this rubbish strike, someone who applied for maternity leave would be ready to resume work." My body stiffens.

I force myself to shrug and steady my voice.

"There has been no news yet, Daddy," I say.

In my prayers this morning, I begged God to extend the strike, to ensure that no university voted that the strike be suspended. I need time to figure out my mess and at least allow myself to heal from the abortion.

"I pray they start soon. We need to be putting these things in our prayers. With the way Nigeria is now, only God can save us."

I nod and start walking away from the living room, from my father and his hopeful gaze. When I enter my room, I settle on a heap of clothes and cry. How did I allow myself to get pregnant?

In the past, I had imagined what it would feel like to be pregnant, to stand before a mirror with swollen breasts, a round protruding belly and slender hips. I imagined wearing a brown pencil gown the same colour as my skin so that I could appear naked from far away. I look in the mirror now and cry. I am wearing red Palazzo trousers and a black tank top. My phone is in my hand and I am searching for a good clinic. There are a lot of DIY tips on blogs detailing how to self-abort a pregnancy.

My phone rings with Davido's husky voice blaring out and I flinch. It is a call from a customer.

"Hello, am I speaking with *Glam Girl*?" I can hear an edge to the voice. I sit up. I had always admired my father as a businessman. I watched him whenever I followed him to his shop at Balogun where he sold all sorts of shoes. I saw how much grit he showed, how much resilience. He had told me that the secret to success was consistency, will, skill and confidence. I believed him. I believed anything he said. It was Daddy. A part of me knows that I started *Glam Girl* to show I had some sort of skill.

"Yes," I clear my throat. "*Glam Girl* here."

"Aunty, when will I get my order? You promised that I would get it this week."

"You will," I say quickly, wiping my tears with my free palm. "Delivery takes three to five working days, like I stated. I have sent out the orders, the dispatch rider will get to you in due time, please." "Hmm, I need the hair before Saturday, abeg."

"It is still Tuesday," I say, rolling my eyes. "It will get to you."

She is silent for a while. Then she makes a guttural sound and hangs up. Usually, after a call like this, I would call Belema to rant, or even Tobore. But today, I have bigger problems.

My phone vibrates. It is a message from Belema. She has sent the location of a clinic, Angel's Point. I stare at it for a while. She calls not long after this.

"Petite," she says, her voice stern, "We have to go to this place. They are tested and trusted."

I do not doubt her. I do not doubt anything at this point, but I wonder where I would get a hundred thousand naira from within such a short time. I have about a quarter of that in my account. Asking Nelson or even Daddy for money would raise suspicion, especially since I am not in school.

"What do you need the money for? I gave you money last week," Nelson would say. Daddy would laugh it off and tell me to ask Nelson. Mummy would be suspicious. Sobenne's job at the bank is not paying her well enough for me to ask her for money.

I want to scream in frustration. The only way to get that money within the next two days would be by selling at least two to three virgin human hairs, or a bone straight.

"Let us wait till the end of this week. I will give you an update by then," I assure Belema.

"Alright, no wahala. I dey for you," she reminds me like she always does. I whimper, because I am certain that I do not deserve this love. I do not deserve Belema. I do not deserve this much support. After all, this pregnancy is my fault. It was I who messed up.

"Thank you so much," I whisper.

"You should call them sha. I will send their number. It is good to enquire down."

We end the call and I start tidying up the room so that I can set up the ring light and create some hair content for Instagram and WhatsApp. The pregnancy test strips I used are still beneath the bed where I slid them in some days ago when I suspected that someone was coming. I have been too scared to dispose of it after that. But I need to do so soon enough before Sobenne finds it there while searching for one of her shoes.

3

It is Friday evening and I am in the living room. Sobenne has complained that I have been quiet for the last few days. She asks if I am ill, depressed or going through something. I dread the day I would start vomiting, running to the toilet in the early hours. I remind myself of how much money I have to make to be able to get rid of the pregnancy. Belema advises that I tell Tobore. He is after all the father. She is sure that he would support me. But I do not want him involved. I have been avoiding his calls for days, giving him one-word responses and snapping at him because I want him to leave me alone.

"Nne, a penny for your thoughts?" Mummy asks, picking up the TV remote from the marble side table.

"Nothing," I say quickly, adjusting on the couch. Mummy's thoughts seem to have shifted elsewhere. The overhead light illuminates her light skin and it looks aureate.

"I hope this light lasts," she says, looking up at the chandelier.

The electricity company has been kinder than usual recently. I am sure that, with elections imminent, the government is trying to butter up Nigerians. The light reflects off the white living room walls so that the room dazzles and the gold couch and blue LED lights that line the edges of the wall stand out. The Virgin Mary statue stands on the three-layered shelf beside the television. A rosary hangs around her neck. I recite the rosary prayer in my head. As I stare at it, I wonder if she is disappointed in me. I look away at my phone. It sits on my thighs, but I do not want to touch it because then mummy will begin to complain about how much we *press* phones these days and how outrageous it is.

Sobenne sits beside me, staring into her phone, her large lips pulled up yet scrunched. She is trying to hide her grin. She must be seeing someone.

Daddy breaks into a song as he descends the stairs. He is clapping as well and I smile.

"Zee Nwa, Zee Nwam o..." Daddy sings. He must be a step or two from the living room entrance now because his voice sounds so close. I rise and move toward his voice.

"Nnam a bia wa lam o," I sing back. Daddy is in the living room now and we are dancing toward each other. Mummy looks at us, a small smile on her face. Daddy is dancing, moving his feet, swaying his hips poorly and clapping his hands as he sings and calls out to me. He is a tall man; I think he used to be taller. I heard that when you reach a certain age, your height shrinks a little. After Nelson, Daddy is the tallest in the house. There was a time when Daddy still towered over us all and I used to look up to see his face and scream, "Giant!" between giggles. He would then swoop me into his arms and I would stare down at the ground, and I would shriek, thrilled to be far from the earth. I dance towards him now. My heartbeat slows and allows me to bask in the moment, in the love and comfort that my daddy offers.

This singing and dancing between Daddy and I is routine, to the envy of other family members. Daddy calls for me in a song, praises me in Igbo and then we hold each other and laugh in the faces of everyone else. Sobenne often tries to do hers with mummy, but mummy is stiff and she does not express herself well with music. There is an image of her already etched in my mind. It is of her in a suit, pumps, glasses, red lips and a stern expression. I think her career as a teacher has a lot to do with that image.

"Baby and daddy have started again," Sobe says. She then stands up, her thighs jiggling as she rises. She is wearing a short jean skirt that hugs her wide hips and a tank top that outlines her large boobs. Sobenne got the good genes, the womanly genes, while I got small boobs and narrow hips. When we walk together, no one believes that we are related. She runs towards us and joins us in dancing. She giggles as she does this, flashing the gap in her tooth.

"Let me even join and dance today. Daddy hail me too o," she demands.

Laughter fills the air. Daddy calls her name as he sings, beckoning her to dance for him, to twirl. He begins to switch between our names. Mummy giggles from where she is. Sobenne dances so well, breaking her ukwu like a real Ada, bending her back and shaking her shoulders, unlike me. As she settles into the dance, all attention now on her, I take the time to step aside and watch. Mummy is no longer seated; her favourite sitcom is now abandoned. She hails Sobe. Her stiff dance moves set in. I laugh.

"Ada m! Give us!" Mummy hails.

"Sobe baby!" I hail too, but my mind has begun to drift away. Daddy may never call me to dance with him again if he finds out about my pregnancy. Mummy might never flash me her rare smile again. My heart begins to race, and the white walls blur. The paintings on the wall zoom out. The voices begin to grow distant. The gush of blood pumping in my heart fills my ears. I feel as though I am shrinking. My chest closes up and I begin to heave.

I slip away. I feel my way to the empty bedroom beside the kitchen. I close the door and rush into the bathroom. I pour water over my head and just sit there. I leave the tap running and begin to cry, the water drowning out my whimpers.

I think about the clinic, Angel's Point. I have to get to them soon. I have to get the money and just go so that the day I go there is the day I abort the damn foetus.

My phone rings and I see Tobore's face on the screen. I cry and watch the phone ring until it stops. The screen lights up again and the phone begins to ring again. I cry and stare at Tobore's picture on the screen. He sent me pictures earlier from a trip to visit his family in Abuja. In the picture, he wears a pink shirt. His hair is shaved bald and the glimmer on his left ear is from a stud. He looked so fine, breathtaking, and bad-boyish and I liked it.

I am staring at Tobore's picture and I begin to feel guilty. I turn off the tap and answer the call. At the same time, I hear a knock on the bedroom door.

"Midnight call?" I whisper into the phone, my voice shaky.

"Zim," Sobenne calls out.

"Twelve. Don't sleep." I whisper into the phone and hang up.

"Zim, are you good?" Sobenne calls.

I walk out of the restroom to meet her. Only the light from the corridor reaches inside so she cannot make out my face.

"Are you fine?" Sobe asks. She touches my neck. I see her bushy brows creased. She has not carved her brows in months. I move away from her, evading her cold hand.

"I'm fine," I say.

She eyes me. She is about to say something when we hear Nelson's voice. His voice is so deep and audible he does not need to shout to be heard. His voice carries from the living room to the bedroom and it is as though he is with us in the room. Sobenne rushes out to the living room. I exhale loudly and follow behind her.

Nelson stands under the chandelier, in track pants and a black shirt. His hair and beard look freshly trimmed. He towers over everyone, his shoulders broad, and his biceps bulging. We share the same dark skin, red lips, narrow noses, full cheeks, and large eyes with scanty lashes. Nelson and I look so alike that people assume I am his daughter when we walk together.

I do not go to embrace him like Sobe or to stand around him like the parents. Nelson sees me as the experimental child with whom to practice fatherhood and I hate it. Even Daddy was never as strict with Nelson as Nelson is with me. I choose not to embrace him whenever he visits. I instead say a short greeting and side-hug him, then retreat and wear a plastic smile. I do not do even that anymore.

"Zimife," he calls out from where he stands, one hand in his pocket.

His eyes look fiery when he looks at me. I know I annoy him for not skipping around him like the rest of the family do.

Unsatisfied, I make him angrier.

"Jigidem," I call back.

I know he hates his native name, the memory that comes with it, the stories we had been told about it. Daddy said Nelson was a frail baby and the doctors said he would die, but Daddy was confident that he would not. Mummy was terrified. In her bid to assuage him to live, she named him Jigidem. *Hold on to me forever.* Daddy said it was the name that saved him. Nelson grew to hate his traditional name.

He clenches his jaw and stops himself from responding. Instead, he smiles at Mummy, ignoring me. I roll my eyes. Daddy and Sobenne give me a look. They always expect me to be grateful to Nelson, irrespective of how badly he behaves.

"Are you spending the weekend?" Mummy asks as she guides him to take a seat. Daddy sits on the couch closest to the steps, so his back is to me. Sobenne sits beside Daddy.

"I will stay here for the weekend and next week," Nelson affirms. Mummy laughs and hugs him. He smiles.

Nelson lives in an apartment in Lekki Phase One. I have only been there once. He lives there because it is closer to the hospital at Victoria Island where he works as a clinical pharmacist. Before then, he had worked at a pharmaceutical. Nelson has been selfsufficient since he graduated from the university. His success has been rapid and with ease. Good things came to him easily. His career has grown smoothly and our parents are always proud of him. He voluntarily assumed all financial responsibility concerning me, since this was the only major financial duty my parents had left. Sobenne was done with school, and we no longer paid rent since we now lived in our house.

"Let Sobenne bring food for you. She cooked beans, your favourite," Mummy gestures to the kitchen. Nelson plumps down beside her and shakes his head slightly.

"Don't stress, Mama. I had dinner at the Oriental before coming here."

"Of course," I mumble. I feel dizzy again, and I find the spectacle even more irritating, so I turn to leave.

"Zimife," Nelson calls after me. I stop and turn towards him. He raises his eyebrows. "What is the update with this strike? Do they plan to call it off anytime soon?"

"Doesn't seem so, at least not from their last meeting. The government is still owing ASUU and they have refused to pay," I say. Nelson shakes his head. He turns to the TV.

"You that you are supposed to finish this year, normally, you are still in your third year. And now it doesn't look like there is much hope."

"Yeah," I agree with him. I regret not agreeing to change to a private school when Nelson had insisted on it in my second year when a strike was declared at the time. Although that strike lasted only two months, it slowed down my schooling.

"We can still work out changing your school," he says, leaning back into the couch and turning towards me. Then he frowns.

"You look pale."

I freeze. My heart begins to pound.

"I'm fine. Just tired. I was about to go to sleep when you called me back," I say as calmly as I can. Nelson eyes me. Mummy squints at me and frowns because she does not like my tone. Daddy continues to watch the television, saying nothing. Sobenne is lost in her phone.

"I'll go to bed now," I say and turn away, hastening up the stairs.

"Someone that will set up ring-light and start making content for Instagram," Mummy jokes.

Sobenne chuckles, it is distant but I hear it. "It is for her business, Mum."

"I know. I like how she is consistent with it."

"What she needs to do is finish school and get a good job, so she can be making proper money. All these businesses—hair or whatever—it's not sustainable in the long run," Nelson says and clears his throat.

"I doubt that. It is how you plan yourself and make use of your profit that determines your growth. Is it not Zim that sold hair worth over a hundred thousand to your mother's friend one day like that? Business is good for her o," Daddy chips in. I smile from where I am eavesdropping at the top of the stairs. Daddy supports me and he always defends me whenever my matter arises, wherever he might be.

"Well, with the strike, she needs something like that," Mummy says.

"There are a lot of other things she can do. She can apply for internships in companies. She can upskill herself in data science, product design and the like. There are so many, so I don't see the point of her sitting around idle, selling hair. It is not a proper career, that's all I'm saying."

I almost shout, 'Wahala' from where I am out of view. Nelson knows how to get at me and he is doing it. Maybe he knows I'm within earshot and just wants to call me out. I continue to the bedroom and lock the door behind me, grateful that everyone is busy downstairs. I am certain Sobenne, with all the distractions surrounding her, would take a while before coming to the room. I sit on the bed and dial Tobore's number. He picks up on the first ring.

"Zim," he says, dragging my name with a loud exhalation, his voice lethargic as always. Tobore speaks as if he is always at rest, unagitated by anything, irrespective of how much stress he is enduring at any time. Once, when we had only started to speak frequently with each other, I asked if he was tipsy. He had been drinking wine and dragging his words. But he was not drunk. It is how he speaks.

"Jesus, I've been trying to get to you for a long time," he said.

"I've been busy. Swamped. A lot of things, really: attending to orders, trying to create content and stuff like that," I said.

"That's crazy. You've been ignoring all my texts and calls. It feels like a miracle that you even called back." There is a gruffness to his voice that thrills me. It brings back memories of when we were thumping against each other on his bed, gripping sheets, panting as our bodies reacted to the thrusts. That voice, that gruffness, had whispered in my ear in the heat of the moment and this familiar thrill had been there.

"It is," I say, clearing my throat as if to clear my mind.

"Look, if there is something wrong, you can tell me." He sounds like he is stretching. "Because it feels like you want to ghost me and shit like that."

He is right. I want to ghost him. But I think of what Belema said. Tobore can help. Especially if he knows it is his child. I am scared and exhausted. Tobore's voice brings me some comfort. It has for a long time.

"Zim, what is it?"

I start to cry. My palms are sweaty and I rub the right one on the bedsheet and then switch the phone from hand to hand to do the same for the other palm.

"Tobore, I'm pregnant," I whisper. There is a short silence.

"Did you take a test?" He asks finally.

"How else would I have known if I didn't take a test?" I snap.

"Hey, hey, Sissy, calm down," His voice is soothing, unruffled. "We are going to figure this out." He sighs.

"I did not think that small break would matter so much. We should have taken precautions," he said.

My tears begin to cascade down my face and the sobs get louder. I clamp my hand over my mouth to muffle them.

"Hey, if this is why you have been scared, you need to calm down."

"Calm down? My parents will kill me," I cry. "How did I even get myself here?"

"What do you want to do? Whatever your decision is, I'll support you." He still sounds so calm. I do not know how to feel about his response. What do I say? What does he want?

"You would support me even if I want an abortion? What about what you want?"

"Honestly, I'm not in the right space to raise a child now, but we can try to do so. I'm honestly scared of abortions."

"This is not about you," I snap. "You are not the one who would go about with a big belly and get judged, or have to stay back if school resumes, or even have to skip a whole year, who would be a disappointment to her family and have to breastfeed and care for this child. Plus, I am not mentally and financially ready to raise this child."

"Sissy, please calm down. I never said I would force you into keeping it." There is an edge to his voice now.

"Your body, your choice."

This is what I want to hear, right? Why then do I feel a cold wash over me? Why does my body shake when he utters those words? I imagine my vagina bleeding, my intestines twisted, my body frail, down—dying. I shudder.

"Sissy, can you hear me?"

"Yes, yes," I say. I do not want my horrible imagination to stop me from what I am going to do.

"I know a clinic at Yaba. Angel's Point. I hear they are good with abortions. But I need about 100k."

"I genuinely don't have up to that right now. Can you wait till next week? I am expecting some returns," he says.

"I have about 25k." I stand up from the bed and walk to the window. It is dark outside, and the light from our neighbour's house reflects on the tree, but the birds are not there. The branches just sway. "I just need a little help."

"Ok, when do you intend to go?"

"I don't know," I say, sniffling. "I have to come up with a cogent reason for my family for why I might return home late on that day."

"Just tell them you have an economics conference to attend. Make it about your education," he suggests. I like it. "There is a conference of sorts at VI."

"Send me the flyer," I say, turning away from the window. I hear a knock on the door. "I'll talk to you later. Thank you so much." I end the call and rush to the door to unlock it. Sobenne stands there, frowning.

"This one you are locking door," she says.

"I need privacy."

"Well," she grins, her eyes widen. "I have good news!"

"I see that." I smile. She dances into the room, shaking her hips and laughing hysterically.

"Nelson has booked us a family dinner on Wednesday. At Eko Hotel. From work, I dey go that side straight." My mind races. That could be a good time to do what I want to do when everyone is out having fun. They would be too consumed in their fun to notice my absence.

"Really? That's so odd. I have an event. For economics practitioners. At UNILAG," I say, feigning a slight disappointment.

Sobenne frowns.

"From when to when?" She asks.

"Tuesday to Thursday," I say. I say smoothly. "I have to attend. I feel like without school, I am running mad in this house. I stay at home all day doing nothing."

Sobenne's face softens. She touches my shoulder and squeezes lightly. She leads me to my bed and we both sit down.

"I understand," she says, placing her hand on mine. "I spent five years studying mass communication at UNN. Federal schools can disgrace somebody."

"I am just really tired," I sigh loudly. I feel so tired. I wish I could share this burden that weighs on me.

"Don't worry, jare, it is not by how fast but by how well. With Nelson working at that big hospital, he surely can get you a good-paying job like he did me." I rear my head and stare at her.

"Is that your job good-paying?" I ask sarcastically. She bursts out laughing and I join her.

"It is not, but he thinks it is—in a Nigeria where most of us are self-employed."

"Are you still looking for work in the media? Where to write and show how creative you are?" I ask, concerned. Sobenne sighs and nods.

"You know I am."

"You will get it soon," I affirm. I know she would. She is an exceptional writer and she would be terrific in the media. Sometimes we lie in bed discussing her ideas. Most of the TikTok and Instagram content for *Glam Girl* that gets so much engagement on my page are her ideas.

"Amen!" She cries out and then kisses my cheek. I feign irritation. She laughs and holds on to me tight, the air grows solemn.

"I also pray for you, my small girl, your business will grow, and, more than anything, you will be able to stand on your feet." That is all I want.

4

When I sit through communion, I think of Jaja in *Purple Hibiscus*. Maybe Daddy would think me rebellious like Jaja's father did him. I imagine a figurine flung toward me, falling and shattering to pieces. But we have no figurine, and I cannot imagine Daddy hitting me. The smell of vinegar—the blood of Jesus—wafts in the air. The scent is so strong that I feel nauseous and dizzy.

"Can you smell this vinegar? It smells so strongly today," I say to Sobenne, who has returned from taking her communion and now sits beside me. Her orange fascinator covers part of her face, so she raises her head slightly to look at me. The hymn is ending so the choir raises their voices harmoniously. Sobenne shakes her head.

"How can you even smell it? The altar is all the way there." She gestures to the altar, which is four pews away from us.

I do not respond. I caution myself from talking too much. My sense of smell is strangely heightened. I swallow and focus on the altar. The mosaic of the Virgin Mary behind the altar glares at me. I look away quickly.

Nelson sits beside Mummy who sits beside Daddy on the second pew. They meet the Priest after the mass so that Nelson can make a big donation to the new church building. Mummy has convinced him, and Daddy supports her. Nelson had been reluctant. He does not particularly believe in the church, but he does believe in God. He has made this clear in the recent past. Mummy believes that work consumes him too much, so he now talks rubbish.

True to his word, Nelson stays through the week. I plan to visit Angel's Point on Wednesday. Tobore says he would be ready then. I tell everyone at home I have a conference to attend, and share a flyer with them, but I have twitched the location and replaced it with the Multipurpose Hall at UNILAG.

Everyone is excited about Nelson's proposed dinner. Sobenne spends her nights selecting what to wear and asking what I think about each outfit. Daddy and Mummy dance about going on a date. Nelson sits in the living room and gives instructions on how everyone should enjoy themselves.

As Wednesday draws near, I begin to have nightmares. In one, a strange man in a white lab coat sticks a gloved hand into my vagina until blood flows out and pain courses through my body. In another, I am crying and crying until my body gives way. Belema calls to check up on me. She insists she will go with me to Angel's Point. She asks that I tell Tobore about this and I do.

Tobore checks up on me as well. I stay longer on the call with him. He tells me about work, how starting a fintech company in Nigeria is not easy and how he is pushing through with his team. His company has been in the works for years and now that they finally launched, a lot is happening all at once; and while that is good, he has to be careful to navigate it well. The company was the reason he had held off his youth service for a while, and now he would be done in a month. He can then focus on his own company. He often ends the call with something like *Make it a great night* or *Sleep well, Sissy* or *Dream about me.*

On Wednesday morning, Sobenne leaves for work after prayers. Mummy and Daddy also leave for work. The house is quiet and I cannot find Nelson anywhere so I presume he has left for work as well. This gives me enough time to prepare before Tobore comes to pick me up. He lives at an estate in Abijo, not too far from my house.

It is past nine and I am dressed. I wear a yellow knee-length dress, which Belema gave me on my last birthday, and a pair of white sneakers. I have not had an appetite to eat. My throat keeps closing up and my stomach is unsettled. I go to the kitchen to drink water. I open the back door and the windows for air to come in. I am in the middle of opening a sachet of water when my phone rings. I retrieve my phone from my purse to answer the call. It is Tobore.

"You here yet?" I ask, placing the sachet of water on the kitchen slab. His voice is scrambled and this irks me.

"Can you hear me?" I ask. "What sort of rubbish network is this?" I say under my breath.

"Yeah, yeah. Can you hear me now?" He says, and then his voice breaks again. I sigh in exasperation and place the phone down and on speaker.

"Tobore."

"I can hear you now," he says. His voice is clear now. "I was saying that you need to resend the address and directions. You say it is after Blenco?"

"Yes," I say, nodding, then I start giving him directions.

"Okay, okay. I'll be there in a few minutes"

"This uncle, be fast o."

"I am not the one you are talking to," he says. I smirk.

"As per what, are you not an uncle?"

"Not yours," he says quickly. "That would be incest. You and your uncle cannot be making babies."

I guffaw. His words are so sudden they amuse me. I feel a tingle in my chest and I shake my head.

"That made you laugh," he says quietly. He sounds distant like his mind is elsewhere.

"I have to get rid of this foetus."

"I know. I am pro-your choice. Whatever you want."

"Thank you. Get here fast so we can get this over with and I can forget that I ever carried anything."

"That would be good."

"This abortion is for the best," I say, more to reassure myself than him. I do not know if I regret what I am about to do, or if it is the fear of something going wrong, but my heart pounds and I feel a slight pain.

A shadow covers my hand on the kitchen counter. Startled, I turn around toward the back door. Standing there heaving and glaring at me is a sweaty Nelson.

"Zim?" Tobore calls. I am frozen.

"Zim... Can you hear me?" I scamper to grab the phone and hang up.

Nelson stares down at me, heaving. His red track pants and black singlet are damp, so they stick to his body.

"You did not go to work," I blurt. I cannot stand on my own so I lean against the counter. I become dizzy. I giggle nervously.

"You are pregnant, Zimife." He looks at my belly.

"I can't—" I stop talking, snatch the sachet of water from the counter, and squeeze all the water into my mouth so fast I sputter. I am nauseous. My palms are sweaty.

Nelson is shouting but I cannot hear him anymore. All the heaviness suddenly disappears and I feel so light I could be blown away. I feel myself fading and all the lights suddenly go out.

5

I hear a distant beeping and I remember movies where a patient lies in bed, tubes connected to her face, arms, and wrists. I open my eyes slowly. I see a drip hanging above me on a pole and a tube that runs from it into my left wrist. I wonder what I look like to an onlooker. The room smells of medicines and disinfectant. I am suddenly uncomfortable. The walls are so white the brightness blinds. My eyes dart about to the clock on the wall opposite me and the windows on the right. At the door, I see two people whispering to each other. I squint and see that it is Belema and Ned.

It is as though my insides are somersaulting; my throat feels like it is holding something heavy. Belema smiles at something Ned says to her. She looks downcast and he seems to be trying to comfort her. I am too weak to move and too shocked to speak and watching them discomforts me. Ned is Belema's boyfriend and I have not seen him in about a month.

I have known Ned since secondary school. At the time, I had a stupid crush on him. He was a senior, a pretty boy, light-skinned with pink lips and sleepy eyes that made it seem as though he was staring at you seductively, which made many junior girls fawn over him. Even now, as a twenty-three-year-old, he is a good-looking man. His jaws are more defined and he keeps a moustache and beard now. With his sleepy eyes, he looks more like an exhausted man.

He and Belema met a year ago at a business hangout in Lekki Phase One. Belema had encouraged me to attend, for my business' sake, and offered to accompany me. That was when I saw Ned again for the first time since we left secondary school. I introduced him to Belema. We talked for a bit, but he talked more with Belema. He complimented her hair, her dress, her skin—everything about her. Passersby made comments about them giving birth to an albino or an *Oyinbo* baby. *Una too fine; make una marry; una fit well well.*

They began dating two weeks later. Ned and I were not so close before then, but when they began dating, we spoke a bit more. Ned is older by a year and attended a private university. He graduated last year and is currently a youth corps member at an oil company in Lagos. I watch him now lean in to hug Belema, and my body begins to act funny. My palms are sweaty, but I cannot rub them against anything, so I stay still, watching them.

His eyes meet mine as he hugs Belema, but I look away, up at the ceiling. A force rises to my throat and I lean over the bed and disgorge onto the floor. When I raise my head, I find Belema beside me already and I hear Ned running off to call for help—a nurse, a cleaner, I don't know. Belema helps me stand up from the other side of the bed and follows me to the bathroom, wheeling the IV fluid hanger behind me. I rinse my mouth at the sink and vomit some more.

She rubs my back in the dim bathroom, telling me sorry, asking if I still feel like vomiting. When we return to the room, an angry-looking woman is cleaning up my vomit.

"How did I get here?" I ask. My head aches. Belema looks at me and shakes her head slowly.

"Petite, Tobore called me to rush down here."

I frown, trying to recall what had happened. My mind has been so consumed by Ned's presence. My knees feel wobbly and I just want to sit down. I start to recall. Tobore, Angel's Point and then... Nelson. I gasp and turn to Belema and grip her baggy shirt by its hem, my eyes wide.

"Belema! Nelson. He was there. He knows." Belema is nodding, her lips turned down and her eyes sullen.

"Petite... your dad is in the lobby with Nelson and Tobore. They have been arguing since we got here."

I want to sit down and catch my breath. I cannot feel my legs again. My knees buckle and I nearly fall, but Belema holds me. She does not say a word as she helps me back into the bed. My eyes water. I look out the window and all I see are the clouds. This building must be very high.

"Where is this?"

"We are in VI. It is the hospital where your brother works."

I open my mouth to speak but I can only nod. My body is shaking and my eyes feel like a fountain. I imagine that all this is a movie or a dream. The door opens and I see that it is not. The cleaner leaves and the room smells refreshed with disinfectant. I feel nauseous again. A nurse comes in to check on me. She says I am fine: I just need to sit and allow the rest of the fluid in the drip to go into my wrist. Ned comes in after the nurse leaves, and Tobore comes in behind him. I see Tobore and everything stills. He strolls toward me. The shirt he wears does not hide the fact that he has gained a bit of weight. His cheeks are fuller, his skin a bit lighter and his lips plumper. His beard is slightly overgrown. I like his glow; he looks really good. His doe-like eyes focus on me and I feel a charge surge through me. Behind him is Nelson. I do not see Daddy and I cry harder.

Ned shoves his hands into the pockets of his jeans and goes to stand beside Belema. Nelson stares me down and I wonder what he is thinking. He must think I am a disgrace, a dent to his great plan, a loose younger sister. I cry harder.

Nelson is wearing suit pants and a blue shirt now. Our eyes meet and my sobs calm down. What was he even doing at home? My head tilts a bit as I look at him. Now I am enraged. He was not supposed to be at home. I was supposed to be at Angel's Point now, taking the foetus out. If he had not interfered, all of this would be playing out differently.

Tobore saunters towards me and sits on the bed. My heart skips as this happens. And when he takes my hand and rubs it, it feels as if something is somersaulting inside my chest. Our eyes meet and, in his eyes, I see a swirling. My throat clogs and I look down.

"Don't cry; it would give you a headache," he says. He raised his brow and I wish for him to keep it that way. The memory of lying in his bed, my finger clutching the sheets, hit me and I wonder why these thoughts are in my head at this time.

"That is not comforting," I retort, trying not to smile. He continues to rub my hand, and when he licks his lips, my eyes follow his tongue.

"I know, but it has all happened. We plan from here—"

"I want to talk to my sister alone," Nelson interjected, his voice filling the room. He steps forward from where he is standing. Belema comes to kiss my cheek. Ned nods at me and walks out of the room with Belema. Tobore does not move for a moment. He then rises and walks out at an even pace. Slightly shorter than Nelson, Tobore does not spare him a glance as he walks past him, seeming unperturbed by Nelson's glare.

The room is so quiet now the beeps from the ECG seem to have become louder. I hear footsteps and distant voices in the hallway.

"You went and got yourself pregnant by a struggling tech bro," Nelson started. I inhale deeply and say nothing.

"I cannot believe you would deliberately bring shame to this family. You even wanted to abort the pregnancy! What sort of catholic are you? What happened to all the catechism classes you attended, all the readings and prayers?"

I recall the mosaic of the Virgin Mary and guilt envelops me.

"It was not deliberate. What were you even doing at home?" I look at him now.

He scoffs.

"I was on my day off! I was trying to refresh myself for the dinner."

"The family dinner is that important to you?"

"Do you even know the magnitude of what you've done? Of you being pregnant at this age? What this could mean for your education? Your future career, Daddy, Mummy, me?" He slaps his chest. "Do you know how this affects us? Our long-term plans-"

"My long-term plans," I cut in quietly, looking at the white polish on my toenails, parts of which are chipped.

"You're supposed to be smarter than this, Zimife!" He snaps and I flinch. I refuse to let more tears fall, so I look up to hold it in. The white ceiling has a small streak of brown, perhaps from a past roof leak. This small detail makes it ugly. I imagined being ugly while pregnant and I shudder.

"So, you just go around spreading your legs?"

"Do you not spread yours?" I retort. I regret saying this but I cannot take it back.

"Something must be wrong with you upstairs," Nelson barks at me. "You are not even apologetic. You were not careful and you are not even fazed about how bad this is," he says calmly now, as though too exhausted to yell. But umbrage courses through me. I am livid, so my voice belts when I respond.

"What do you mean I am unapologetic? Unfazed? What does that even mean? Are you in my body? Do you know how shaken I have been in the past week? You are attacking me because you are not the one who is pregnant, not because you are better."

"Watch your—" The door opens and he stops mid-statement and mid-walk. He had taken a step toward me, wagging his index finger. His eyes soften and his shoulders sag.

I turn towards the tall dark-skinned woman who has entered the room. She wears a white lab coat over her blue dress and hangs a stethoscope around her neck. She holds a clipboard and a pen. As she walks into the room, the heels of her black pumps thump the ground. Her tiny eyes dart between Nelson and me, her long lashes fluttering. Nelson has his back to her.

"Hello," she smiles at me. I nod. She removes the stethoscope from around her neck, places the clipboard and pen on the edge of the bed, and walks around Nelson to me.

"How are you?" She asks, smiling.

"Well," I manage to say. She turns to Nelson and sighs.

"Pharm," she says and coughs lightly, "could you give me a moment alone with the patient?"

Nelson sighs, looking defeated. "Sure, sure," he says, then turns and leaves the room. She turns back to me.

"I am Doctor Isioma. I was the one who examined you when you were brought in." I nod, feeling relaxed. A nurse enters and stands beside the doctor, picking up the clipboard Dr Isioma had left on the bed.

"We carried out a couple of tests and you are eight weeks pregnant." She says "eight weeks" slowly, as though to emphasise it. I nod again and she smiles.

"You fainted from exhaustion and stress, and it seems you have not been eating well." She smiles again and I am beginning to hate it.

"Your pregnancy is fine... You are fine."

But I am not, I thought to myself. She examines me: checks my eyes, and my heartbeat, asks if I feel any discomfort, and then asks some other questions that I will not remember. She says I am free to go home once the drip is finished. Before she leaves, I dare to ask.

"Is there any way that I can lose the baby? Is there anything that can cause a miscarriage?" She shakes her head.

"Do not harm yourself. The best way to get rid of a pregnancy you might not want is by getting an abortion. Manual Vacuum Aspiration. Works well for early pregnancies." She says this, quietly, carefully, with a gaze that shows that she knows I cannot go through with it. She knows my elder brother would not let that happen. I look away, she stands for a bit and then leaves.

I curl into a foetal position on the bed and watch the ants form a line on the wall. Later, as we return home in Nelson's Ford, the air is thick with Daddy's silence and the apology I am too petrified to utter. Daddy just stares out the window, only nodding to Nelson's small talk.

I expected him to yell at me or accuse the devil. But this silence, I did not expect it nor know what to do with it. I look out the window. It is night and Lagos is alive with people and lights, the streets glimmering with yellow, white, and neon lights—danfo buses calling for passengers, music blasting from stores and cars, curses in Yoruba flying in the air.

I dread arriving at home. I sit alone in the back and I want this ride to go on forever so that we never have to reach home, where I will have to alight and face everyone: Daddy's wistful gaze, Nelson's frown and the unpredictable ones of Mummy and Sobenne.

When Nelson drives into the compound and parks, the heaviness in my chest worsens. I lean against the car after alighting to steady myself. When I look up, I am alone. Daddy and Nelson have entered the house. It is windy and I wish my hair was long, perhaps braided so that I can feel the wind swinging against it, so that I can feel like a girl from the movies, so that this can make it all easier. I lean away from the car and walk into the house.

My heart skips when I see Mummy standing by the staircase in a bubu gown, holding a paper I suspect reads the pregnancy test result. Sobenne stands beside her, covering her mouth to suppress a gasp or a scream. Mummy raises the paper.

"You are pregnant?" She asks, glaring and shaking the paper at me.

I drop my head. She exclaims. I flinch.

"Under this roof, you have gone eight weeks. Eight! Zimife! Did I raise an *akuna*?"

I raise my face at her sharply, startled. The words cut through me. This is what happens when a girl gets pregnant out of wedlock. She is called all sorts of things. She is called a prostitute. My mother's fury burns through me. I look down and feel the tears coming.

"As small as you are, you are spreading your legs about, ehn! You are having unprotected sex! If it were not pregnancy, it could have been AIDS!" Mummy shouts. I am afraid she will walk over and strike me across my face.

Tears fall on my white-polished toenails. My palms are sweaty and they shake as I rub them against my dress.

"You are a shame, Ozimife. A shame to this entire family, to the whole of Agulu, Umubiala. The entire kinsmen. That you would go and get yourself pregnant without being married, and at this stage in your goddamn life!"

My sobs increase, I just want to be away from here. Away from her words.

"Look at Sobenne. She is much older than you, but she did nothing of this rubbish. Look at Nelson. Have you heard that he brought any woman home pregnant? Who do you emulate with this despicable act? Who are you?" My body shakes. Who am I?

"Tufia!" she flings the test result towards me and storms away. I stare at the paper on the ground a couple of metres away from me.

I am left with Sobenne, and a part of me awaits her reproval. I wonder now what she thinks of me at this time. Perhaps because of the age difference between us and how far apart our growth has been, I did not always feel that I could share the innermost details of my life with her. We have great conversations but I have never felt the freedom to go to the very depth of my soul with her. I wonder now if she is pained that I did not trust her enough to tell her earlier that I was pregnant.

Like Daddy, I fear that she may judge me and that I may never again be her *Baby*.

I wait. My chest feels like it might combust and I cry out loud. I hear Sobenne walking towards me and I am relieved when she wraps her arms around me. She holds on to me and allows me to cry on her bosom.

"Shh, shh... Baby, everything is going to be fine... shh..."

Sobenne holds me and pats my back. She smells of ofe akwu and seasoning powder. She must have been cooking.

She leans away gently and gazes at me softly. "What happened, Zim? How na?"

"It was a mistake," I sob. "It was a mistake."

"If not that you fainted, we would not have known. When Nelson sent the message on the family group chat about you fainting and his suspicions that you are pregnant, I just prayed it was not true."

This means Nelson did not tell anyone that I had planned to have an abortion. A part of me is relieved, even thankful to him. I remember now that he is the reason I have to keep this pregnancy and I am furious again. But now I do not have to worry about judgment for planning an abortion. I am somewhat relieved that, to the rest of my family, my sin is only one.

"So, who is the father?" she asks.

"One guy like that. Tobore."

"Tobore," she whispers and frowns slightly. She rubs my forearm.

"Your boyfriend? I have not heard about this one, last one I heard was about that stupid boy that you were dashing money."

"No...yes. We are not dating. We were still talking—something like that."

"Ah," she frowns, "a situationship." "Sobenne," I sigh.

"It is a situationship, Zimi. If you talk constantly, you are close, and then you now have sex, but there is no label, then you are in a situationship o. Whose fault is the situationship, by the way? Which one of you is resisting a label?" She raises an eyebrow.

I shrug. At one point, Tobore wanted to put a label on it but I was not ready. Then things happened that I just could not place my hand on. We drifted apart a bit even before the sex but it became worse after the sex.

"Should we even be talking about this now?" I ask, taking a step back. I want to go to the room and lie down and cry. I am thinking now of the implications of keeping this pregnancy. I would no longer make Instagram reels for *Glam Girl* because no one can see me this way. Then there is school. I cannot return to school like this when we resume. I hope the strike goes on for a year. It would be outrageous to go to church when my stomach starts protruding when I do not have a ring on my finger. The judgmental gazes I would attract are already making me anxious.

Sobenne entwines her fingers in mine, her smile broad.

"Come on, Baby; come and bath and have some rest. You look tired."

I let her lead me upstairs, her fingers firmly holding onto me.

I begin to climb up the stairs, my feet heavy, my heart heavier.

6

Silence and solitude become my sentencing. Morning prayers become centre stage for my judgment. Daddy has not spoken to me. Nelson has returned to his house. Sobenne's comfort is in what she offers: her shoulders, food, and sympathetic whispers. She calls me on her way back from work to ask if I have any food cravings and if she should buy me burnt bole, suya fat, or hot bread from the bakery. She assumes that I would crave odd foods. It is during those calls she makes, even though she knows that Lagos traffic would make her journey longer and strenuous, that my day brightens. Aside from that, I grow quiet as the days go by. I ignore calls from Tobore, Ned and even Belema.

One Saturday afternoon, when I am in the kitchen with Sobenne, Daddy, in the living room, says something that shocks me. We are preparing ingredients for okra soup. Sobenne chops the panla, while I chop the ugwu leaves. We stand side by side in front of the kitchen counter, the air filled with the smell of ice fish, frozen chicken and ogbono.

"That young man, Tobo-whatever. He should be called for a meeting."

"Is he not the one that Nelson said is still struggling to start a company?" Mummy scoffs. Sobenne stops chopping and looks at me. I look at her as well, shocked.

"Let us know who he is and where he is from. Let us know how Zimife can marry him. No child of mine will bring me disgrace like this."

Daddy never calls me Zimife, but I suspect that is what he will call me henceforth. Zimife. So plain for a daughter who had brought him light.

The thought of having to marry Tobore dazzles me. The thought of being married off so quickly terrifies me. Before this pregnancy, I did not have marriage in my plans and was sure I would not get married until I turned twenty-eight in seven years. But now, it is expected of me. My grip on the knife loosens and it clatters to the floor. Sobenne's gaze averts to it.

"Calm down," she says as she bends to pick up the knife. She places it on the counter. My phone starts to ring. I retrieve it from my pocket and swipe to answer the call. It is a dispatch rider who is supposed to do the rounds of hair delivery today.

"Hello ma, I am in front of your estate now," he says.

"Come on in. I told the gate people that you would be coming."

"Ok, ok. Thank you."

I walk out of the kitchen to the dining area, where the blue branded bags are on the floor against the wall, the orders written on them. I had made a video of the packages earlier and posted them on Instagram and WhatsApp. It has been days since I made a video of myself.

"Bia, Zimife," Daddy calls. I look up, but I can barely see him through the living room entrance, so I stand and walk over to the living room threshold. Daddy wears only cargo shorts as he watches TV. Mummy looks at me through her glasses, her face scrunched up as though she is looking at something that disgusts her.

"This your hair, when you were dyeing it, I said it was your first sign of rebellion. Your father did not listen to me. You will have to dye it back to black. We cannot be dealing with you being pregnant and then carrying dyed hair. Next thing we know, you will pierce your nose or draw tattoos all over your body, then we know that it is all finished and that there is no redemption for you." "Obim," Daddy cautions Mummy.

Mummy stops talking, but she continues to scowl. I rub my palms against the back of my jeans. I feel tears gathering in my eyes.

"That boy, Tobore or whatever his name is. You have to call him to come here. We have to talk to him to know the plans for the future," Mummy says. Daddy nods but he still does not look at me.

"Call him now. We must see him."

I look from Mummy to Daddy, a protest dancing at the tip of my tongue, but I know it would not help my case if an argument ensues. So, I simply nod and go back to what I was doing. When the dispatch rider arrives, I give him all the packages as well as a written list of addresses for delivery. I send him the fare and watch him ride off. I call Tobore right then. He answers on the first ring.

"For fuck's sake, Zimi, what's with you and this habit of ghosting people?"

"Hey," I clear my throat. "My parents want to meet you."

"Zimi," he groans. "Sometimes I don't get you and I don't get what the hell is even going on with you. You ignore everyone and then, when you eventually come around, you expect that everyone just falls in line."

"What are you even saying, Tobore? I am going through a lot and all you can say is that I am what?"

"You are not even apologetic. You just expect the world to be at your beck and call. Look, I know this baby is growing in your belly, but I am involved too. I am the father of that child, remember? The father."

I stare at the wall, irritated by the algae at its base and by Tobore for being upset with me. Maybe I am acting out of order but does he know the things I have been going through, the effect of all this on my mental health, and how exhausting it has been?

"Are you coming or not?"

"Zimife," he says and sighs. "Yeah, I'll come."

"Can you come today?"

"Okay." He hangs up immediately and a lump grows in my throat. I feel guilty for my behaviour towards him. He has been nothing but kind to me. He has called, even though he does not quite like phone calls; he has texted often, offering reassurance; and he has remained calm through it all, until now.

Tobore arrives at my house two hours later. I am the first person to see him because I have been standing outside expecting him, pacing back and forth and leaning against the wall rubbing my palms against my dress. My heartbeat accelerates as I watch him drive his Toyota Camry through our gate. He is wearing a brown two-piece kaftan that makes him seem confident and steady. There are bags beneath his eyes and his hair has grown out of the carved line. I want to touch his face, run my fingers over it and ask if he is all right. But he is far away. Even when he comes close to me, he is unreachable and our eyes averted each other.

The passenger door opens and I turn to see Belema frowning at me. I look down and try to force a smile.

"Is this a gang-up?" I ask as they step closer to me. I giggle nervously and feel a shiver when Tobore finally looks at me. His beard is fuller and I wonder if he intends to trim it or if he wishes for it to keep growing full.

"I'll reboot you now if you don't behave," Belema snaps. She has a septum piercing now. They look nice, but she cannot take this into my father's house, not when my mother suspects that my rebellion started from hair dying and that piercings might follow. If she sees Belema in these purple braids and piercings, she will conclude that Belema is the culprit influencing my bad behaviour.

Tobore looks away and faces the entrance door. I feel his coldness hit me. I wish he would grab my hand so that his thumb can brush the back of my palm.

"Can I go in?" He asks flatly.

"We have to go in together," I say, looking at him.

"Zimi," Belema calls.

"Belema, please wait in the car. Please. Let Tobore and I go in first. I'll call you soon, abeg," I plead.

She looks at Tobore, who gives her a tiny nod and hands her the car key. She turns around and goes back into the car.

Tobore still does not look at me, and with everything mummy said earlier and the baby and everything else going on, his anger towards me hurts. My phone begins to ring. It is a customer and I am certain she is calling to make a complaint. All the weight crushes me and it feels as though all the air has left my lungs and all the tears I had been keeping at bay begin to pour out. My shoulders shake and my head begins to ache. I feel warm hands touch my forearm.

"Hey, Sissy," Tobore whispers and pulls me into an embrace. My arms wrap around him and my body relaxes against his. His chin rests on my head and my face is pressed into his chest, allowing me to inhale him. He smells of perfume and car AC and I inhale him deeply. He lets me cry on his chest without uttering a word, one hand rubbing my back. I want to hold on to this moment.

"I wish I had that abortion, Tobore. It has been hell. My mom does not even care that her words cut so deep. My dad ignores me, my sister pities me. I am the bad egg of this family."

"Shh," he says softly. "Do not talk yourself down. And there's no need to cry. What has happened has happened. Let's just face whatever follows head-on, okay?"

I am calm now and I disengage from him. He is staring down at me, his lips stretched into a smile. I wonder if I should tell him what my parents want to ask him, if I should devise a strategy with him here before facing my parents or if I should wait instead to see what his response would be. Would he agree to marry me? Do I even want him to agree to marry me?

"Sissy," he cuts into my thoughts with a chuckle, "you're overthinking again."

I shake my head and look away, embarrassed by how easily he sees through me. He takes my hand in his and rubs his thumb against the back of my hands.

"Come on, let's go in and hear what your parents have to say." "Yeah." I smile.

We make our way into my home, holding hands. Even as we approach the living room, Tobore does not let go. His thumb begins to rub against my hand and I smile. My heart clumps as we draw near. Just as we are about to walk into the living room, Mummy and Daddy look away from the television and I slip my hand out of Tobore's. He glances at me with a small smile and a gentle nod.

I stand by the door as he walks in and greets my parents. He holds his right wrist with his left hand as he stretches his right hand out for Daddy to shake. Daddy takes his hand in his and shakes it. I am relieved. I know that, as a daughter, I am not supposed to be in the room as they discuss, so I slip out and hide behind the wall so that I can hear their conversation.

"Welcome, nnoo—as our people would say," Daddy begins.

"Dalu," Tobore responds. And, to my astonishment, Daddy lets out a robust laughter. I feel even more relieved.

"You know we are here to discuss Zimife and her pregnancy," Daddy says, clearing his throat, "and with this kind of meeting, I think it is only fitting we break a kola nut, as we do in our land."

I know he will call me to bring the kola nut, so I slip into the kitchen. I am pretending to do something. I open the pots on the cooker and just move around lazily until I hear Daddy call out. It is Sobenne he calls. My stomach twists. She responds on the second call. When I hear the clump of her slippers on the staircase going to fetch the kola nut, I come out of the kitchen and return to my previous position, eavesdropping on the conversation in the living room. Sobenne walks past me without saying a word.

I listen as Daddy says the prayer that the conversation be a peaceful one. Everyone in the living room choruses, "Isee". I do so too under my breath. After a while, Sobenne walks past me again. She goes into the kitchen and I hear her placing tumblers in a tray.

"What plans do you have now that she is pregnant? What do you want to do?" Daddy asks. Tobore clears his throat.

"I intend to be here for her and the baby," he says.

"Yes, you have made that clear at the hospital. But what about her dignity as a woman? In our land, women who are unmarried and pregnant are—" he pauses briefly, "not seen. And this would affect her in the long run."

There is silence. Even Sobenne pauses the noise from the kitchen. I hold my breath and wait for Tobore's response.

"Sir, sincerely speaking, I am not ready to be married at this time. Financially, I am yet to find my feet in this Lagos. Having to be wed would—"

"But you have a child now, what else would drain your money other than your child?" Daddy cuts in.

"Money... the commitment. Marriage is for life, sir. And I am also not certain even Zimife is ready for that at the moment," Tobore responds, picking his words.

"If you both went into a room and conceived a child, then you both might as well get married to each other," Mummy says. Her voice has an edge to it, so it is apparent that the conversation has gotten to the point where it needs her intervention.

"Obim," Daddy sighs. "Look, Tobore. When I married my wife, I did not know who she was. I learnt everything on the way there. And we have grown ever since and are married till now. There is no preparation needed. You will bloom in finance along the way."

"That was then, sir. Things are very different now. I genuinely like your daughter. I just do not have my mind on marriage now. I will be there for Zimife and the baby, but I cannot swear commitment before God and man without knowing and understanding her, without allowing her to do the same about me and without allowing myself to be strong financially." Tobore's response is so measured.

I stand behind the wall, not sure how to feel. Of course, I do not want to get married now, but am I also not worthy of Tobore willing to take the risk? I wonder why he feels that he does not know me. He did, at some point want a relationship, did he not?

I turn away from my hiding place and head outside. When Belema sees me approach the car, she comes out and opens her arms. I walk into them and rest my head on her shoulder. I tell her about the conversation.

"You did say some time ago that you want to get married at twenty-eight when you have gathered money and found the love of your life," she reminds me.

"Yes," I affirm. "I did say so."

"Is he the love of your life?" She asks.

"No, I do not think so. Maybe I'd feel differently if he was... I don't know. But I'm carrying his child," I whisper. "I'd be a baby mama, Belema. A baby mama."

Belema is silent, but I do not feel alone. I know her mind is as burdened as mine. She holds on to me. At this point, I am not certain I know what I want. But I know for sure that if I had succeeded with the abortion, we would not be here in the first place.

My phone beeps and I pull away to look at the screen. It is a message from the number that called earlier. *I was calling to say that*

I got my hair and it is so pretty! I love it! I sigh and smile. I look up at Belema. Her eyes are asking why I am smiling and my eyes are teary. I turn the screen to her. She reads the message and pulls me into her embrace.

7

I do not recall the last time I sat in the living room with my family to watch TV or laugh about anything. I am tired all the time; I wake up to vomit in the morning; I feel aches around my abdomen; my breasts are swollen and painful; my underwear is always wet with discharge that makes me feel uncomfortable. I get hungry at odd hours and have developed odd food cravings, like burnt rice, at inconvenient times. I finish the fruits that mummy stocks in the fridge. I ask for banana bread, which Tobore sends often. I cannot smell evaporated milk. On some days I just want to cry until my eyes fall out. I want to press my leg so it can stop swelling. I want to tie my nose so it stops getting bigger. I want to cut all my hair off.

Every day I wait for it to get worse, so I stay in the shower and let water run down my body and I cry. Tobore is the only person to whom I have tried to be open about this feeling. He suggests, just like Dr Isioma, Mummy and Nelson, that I join some new mothers and pregnancy classes, but I refuse. I think it is a waste of money to sit with women and talk about, what, giving birth?

"You need to take this seriously. Going for these classes can help you a lot," Tobore says.

"Classes that are filled with older married women. I will now go and then feel insulted. I don't like the idea. My chats with Dr Isioma are enough. Plus, the classes mean spending more money."

"Zimi, are you even taking this pregnancy seriously?" He questions. The conversation is over the phone but I wish I could see him frowning. I sit at the dining table eating burnt rice and talking to him on speakerphone.

"What does that even mean?" I snap. "I am carrying the baby now and that is all that matters. If I am not taking it seriously, what can be done about that?"

"Zimi, try to see perspective here."

"Oh, so I'm dumb and single-minded, abi?"

"Well, you are not exactly open-minded about this. You are complaining about something, yet you are dismissing all the solutions being offered." He raises his voice and I wonder why he is annoyed at all. It is not he who has to go to the class and sit between women who have nothing but judgmental thoughts in mind.

"I still don't want the classes. If there are other methods, I'll be thrilled to consider them." I have the urge to add, *And if you like, vex.* But I stop myself.

Tobore sends me articles, Instagram reels and YouTube videos about pregnancy—being a mother, antenatal care, being a new mom, the normalcies. Sometimes, I find them interesting to read and watch, but other times, especially when I am feeling overwhelmed, I ignore his messages. Last week he sent me books about pregnancy and motherhood, but I am not much of a reader, so I keep the books at the bottom of the wardrobe and stare at the closed wardrobe at night. I will pick one of them up one day. I am not certain when, but I will.

It is on one of the days when my mood is dampened that Sobenne catches me. She walks in on me standing beneath the shower, crying. She holds me in the bathroom with her work clothes still on but her wig removed. She allows her body to be drenched as she hugs me, strokes my back and says, "Baby, stop crying. It's okay, Baby. Everything will be okay. You can stop crying now, Baby."

My tears subside. Sobenne asks that we take a walk together. I put on a black bubu dress and my yellow Crocs. Sobenne changes into a blue flare dress that pushes her breasts up but hides her hips, and she wears her black Crocs. She goes to tell Mummy that we are heading out for a stroll. Mummy is busy in her room and Daddy has not returned from work. I hear Mummy's soft hum of acknowledgement.

Sobenne and I walk hand in hand to the park, ignoring the whistlings directed at us, which I am sure are intended for Sobenne.

"I'm just afraid that I may never find love or a partner, you know? I mean, if it's not Tobore, who wants to marry a baby mama? How many baby mamas are even married? I know I didn't want Tobore to say he wanted to marry me, but maybe now I wish he had. My belly is not even big yet, but I can feel people staring at me when I go out or spit in public." I sigh and lower myself onto the yellow concrete seat at the park beneath a masquerade tree.

The estate park is not busy this evening. The masquerade trees sway in the wind, leaves falling through the air. The lawn is almost due for trimming. The sun has just set but it is not dark yet, so the street lights that stare down at the park are yet to be turned on.

"Baby mamas now get married, Zim. Things are changing. At least Tobore did not deny the pregnancy or refuse to support both you and the baby. Hold on to that. Hold on to the fact that he will be a present dad," Sobenne says as she slaps an insect away from her knee.

My phone beeps and it is a text from Nelson reminding me to attend antenatal care later this week at the hospital where he works, as the pregnancy is already twelve weeks old. I tuck my phone away and start to think about what Sobenne said.

Tobore keeps me updated about his company and tells me that his father wants to meet me. Since Tobore lost his elder sister and mother to a car accident when he was a teenager, his father, who lives in Warri, is his only family left.

"Everything na blessing. This child is a blessing. Na bros J do this one for us," his father had said in a voice note Tobore forwarded to me. Tobore has a small inner circle—a small family and a couple of friends—and likes it that way.

My family, on the other hand, is large, and I keep in touch with almost all of them. My father has six sisters and my mother has four brothers, so I have cousins scattered around the world. In my family, news spreads ineffably, so that secrets are always open while still being confidential.

I turn back to Sobenne. "So, I should be thankful for that?"

I scoff.

Sobenne looks up at the tree just as a leaf lands on her shoulder. She dusts it off and nods.

"Yes, you should."

"Because I am a woman who had consensual sex with a man and got pregnant, I should be grateful that he did not deny a child that was conceived from an act that we both committed?" I ask, my voice edgy. A leaf lands on my thigh and I brush it off brashly.

Sobenne's wide eyes meet mine.

"I don't mean it that way, Zim. Of course, it's his responsibility to show up for his baby. What I'm trying to say is, do not let anyone's words push you into not setting your priorities right. I know you'll struggle with the baby mama stereotype and stigma from our baby boomer parents and other people, but you should not fail to recognise who is on your side," she says and leans back.

I smile.

"This is the time to accept fully that certain things happen that should not be held against you. Everything that happened has happened. You owe Tobore nothing and he owes you nothing. The only person you both owe any responsibility to is this child.

"I want you to live in this present, in this reconstruction of meaning, in this reality of self-acceptance that your generation is creating," Sobenne goes on. "Set your priority right in your mind. The baby first, then whatever you want your life to be. Henceforth, you would have to plan with your baby in mind while accomplishing your dreams. I suppose what I've been trying to say is that I want you to know you can do all."

Sobenne smiles and I feel comforted. "I also want you to know that you have family. You have people who love you. You have me. You have Mummy and Daddy, even though they may not show it yet. You have Nelson, you have Belema and then you have that your baby daddy." The wind causes her chiffon dress to swell against her body and her weave to fall over her eyes so that her hands struggle to keep them away.

"I am just saying there are things to be grateful for instead of being gloomy all the time."

I rest my head on Sobenne's shoulder and close my eyes. For the first time in weeks, I feel normal. I have this urge to laugh, to cry, to scream and bask in this surreal feeling. So, I do. Sobenne laughs with me, our bodies vibrating to our laughter.

I want the child in my womb to feel this love, I want my body to feel it, I want to feel like this always. And I will because I know Sobenne is right. First, I have her.

Tobore comes to pick me up for the antenatal checkup wearing a flannel shirt that does not suit him over denim trousers. His haircut is recent, so he looks finer, his features striking. The heat within my body rages so I divert the car air conditioner outlet to my face. Tobore raps along to a Drake song as we leave the estate. He taps his fingers on the steering and dances to the beat as he drives. Then he stares at me and laughs. I watch his fingers and envision them entwined with mine, his thumb rubbing the back of my palm until a soothing consumes my body.

"What is exciting you?" I ask at last.

"My company has secured a kind of big break." He taps his phone which is in a cup holder.

"Help me charge it, please." I plug the phone into the car charger.

"Won't you allow me to share in your joy?"

He nods, reduces the car stereo volume and smirks at me.

"I've finally been able to save up just enough money and have secured a few sponsors to be able to boost my company via a huge platform. And some of the sponsorship money has gone into getting really good web designers to put up a strong website and app. We'd commence Instagram advertisement through a few influencers and then, next year...drum rolls please..."

I drum my hand on the dashboard. Tobore guffaws. His eyes avert to the road. We are in line, waiting for the traffic light to signal a go-ahead.

"I will be advertising on the Big Brother Naija reality show platform!" Tobore announces just as the light turns green and he accelerates the car for effect.

I gasp.

"This is huge, Tobore!" I throw my hands jubilantly in the air.

I know how much this means for his ambition to be a serial entrepreneur and I just feel giddy inside for his success. He stretches his hand and places it over mine. I watch his hand on mine and feel flutters in my heart. I feel warmth inside me, but questions come up and I know that sooner or later, Tobore and I will have to address whatever this is.

The hospital smells faintly of disinfectant, but the reception, a blindingly white room, smells of strawberry and air-conditioned breeze. Few people are waiting, and an enceinte woman stands at the far end of the room, her eyes teary, her hands on her knees shaking. A man comes forward and gently guides her through a door on the right. I hear her scream almost immediately and I shudder. Tobore touches my arm lightly. He nods at the airport seats in front of the receptionist's desk. We walk there and sit.

I spot Nelson when he enters the reception through an inner door wearing a sparkling white lab coat. He nods so slightly at me when our eyes meet before disappearing through another door. I imagine he is embarrassed to be associated with me.

I feel Tobore's gaze on me, but my gaze remains on the television hung high on the wall beside the receptionist's corner. "You don't look like you sleep well. Your eyes are dull," he says. I shrug, not looking at him.

He turns away, looking around the room. I want his eyes back on me and I wish I could reach out to turn his face back to me. I wonder what it is we are even doing. Who is he to me and where is this headed, whatever *this* is? I wonder if anything else is growing between us other than this child growing inside me that binds us to each other. Are we simply co-parents, or are we still in a *situationship*?

The problem with situationships is that they are nearly impossible to define. So, you cannot break what was never solidly in place and I feel frustrated.

"Mrs Ike-Steven?"

I snap out of my reverie. Shocked and afraid, I raise my hand timidly, stand up and walk over to the receptionist. Tobore follows behind, but I hear his phone ring, so he turns around to answer the call.

The receptionist, her eyes trailing Tobore as he moves away, hands me a form and a pen with which to fill it.

"Is that your husband?" She asks. I look up at her and shake my head.

She frowns and looks down. "But he is the father?"

I turn to look at Tobore, who is still on a call, and then I look at the receptionist. I avert her gaze and respond in a low voice.

"Yes."

She shakes her head, and nods at the form, gesturing for me to continue filling it.

My hand starts to shake as I fill out the form, my handwriting haphazard like a polygraph test result. I feel her gaze on me, scrutinising and judging. When I am done, I push the form towards her. She sniffles mildly and skims it. She tsks as she drops it atop a pile of papers on her table. I feel my knees shake and my palms sweating. Tobore approaches us then and the receptionist's face transforms to smile brightly at him.

"Just go left, you will see the door sign, Ob—" I block her words out, and allow Tobore to lead me away from her.

My mind is muddled and I feel myself shaking. I swallow as we walk on, wondering how much judgment lies ahead for me. I turn to Tobore.

"Did you see how that lady behaved to me and changed when she saw you?"

Tobore looks back but keeps walking. "How did she behave to you?"

"I don't know. She eyed me and shook her head and was just judging me. She wasn't even hiding it." My voice breaks as I speak. We are in front of the door now. Tobore pauses and faces me.

"I must have missed it. Just don't dwell on what you think you saw. Don't mind her at all."

Tobore's words, rather than comfort me, make me angrier. All I want is someone who would understand and join me in being angry, who could understand how that woman made me feel and why I can't simply swat it aside. And I want to express all of this, but Tobore knocks on the door. When we walk in, Dr Isioma sits behind the desk and I feel relaxed.

On our way from the hospital, I ask Tobore to drop me off at Agungi Bus Stop, because I want to visit Belema. She had seemed distant during our recent chats. As I make to open the car door to alight, Tobore grabs my left hand. I turn to face him and he stares at me so tenderly that I feel my insides muddle up. I stare at all of him and my heart thuds.

"Please don't let that receptionist woman get to you," he says. I nod rapidly.

"Or anyone else for that matter. Please." I nod again.

He leans in and kisses my cheek. A warmth washes over me and my hand slips off the door handle. I sit still, wanting more. I catch myself and proceed to alight quickly. I stand outside, staring at Tobore through the wound-down window and wave as he drives away, catching myself again and dropping my hand quickly. The heat the peck stirs up within me lingers as I flag down a keke to take me to Belema's neighbourhood. As I walk into Belema's street, I simply nod at Ochuko when he hails me from his balcony, and I have barely stepped into Belema's house before I start babbling.

"You would not believe—" I stop mid-sentence, startled to find, sitting alone on the black couch in a black outfit, Ned. His phone is pressed to his ear and is speaking in a thick delta-Igbo dialect of which I can only make out some of the words. My palms are sweaty but I do not rub them against my dress—it is a bright yellow and I fear that it may get stained if I do.

Ned soon ends the call and settles his soft gaze on me, conjuring to the surface a memory that haunts me.

"Hi," he says.

"Hi," I say. "I am looking for Belema," I add quickly.

"She stepped out to get something."

"Okay," I say. I am not sure what to do, whether to sit or just wait outside. Being in the same room with Ned after what happened a few months ago sets another ball of emotions inside me. *God, abeg.*

"Sit na, you cannot be standing for long in your condition," he says, then clears his throat.

I turn to him sharply.

"My condition?"

He shakes his head.

"You know what I mean."

"No, I don't. What does that mean?" I raise my eyebrows.

"You just want to pick offence from what I said, Zim." He sighs. "I'm sorry if that sounded offensive. I just mean that you should relax."

"I will wait outside."

"Father Lord," he mutters, throwing his hands up and slapping his thighs. "Look, I know this is about what happened in February," he says, but I have turned to walk out of the room.

"We need to talk about it," he says, adjusting to sit straighter. "We have avoided it for so long that it has eaten us up. And what happens when Belema is with us, in the same space? If we don't settle this, she will figure it out, and I don't want that." My shoulder drops and I sigh.

"I don't want that as well," I say.

"Exactly. I really like Belema but what happened was a mistake."

"Nothing happened!" I slap my palms against my thighs. I immediately look to see if my dress is stained but it is not.

Nothing happened, I repeat to myself.

The day before Valentine's, Belema travelled to Bayelsa when her maternal grandfather died. We had expected her to return on the evening of that day. Ned had already told her to come straight to his place—a two-bedroom detached apartment in Buenavista Estate at Orchid Road—upon her return. He wished to do something romantic for her, so he asked me for help. I went there in the morning to help pick out her favourite things in her favourite colours.

After we had finished decorating, we shared a bottle of wine to relax. We sat side by side in the living room, reminiscing our secondary school days. We were laughing about a teacher nicknamed "Bottom Bell" when we both fell on his blue rug. We laid there with our bodies touching, our faces so close I felt his breaths on my face. And just as our noses touched, he pulled back and rolled away from me. We both sprang up into an air of torturous guilt. I promptly wished him good luck with his romantic gesture for Belema and left. He texted to say *Thanks* later. I called Tobore then and agreed to a proposal he made a week earlier to have lunch at his house on Valentine's Day.

Ned stands up now and shoves his hands into his trousers pockets. I had been lost in my thoughts and only started to listen to what he had been saying.

"...so, we should be cool. Let's learn to be friends again, please. For B's sake."

I look up to meet his gaze and nod. Dr Isioma's words at the hospital come to mind now. *Don't worry, after the twelfth week, all the first trimester symptoms and distress begin to subside and you'll see that everything will start to get better from here on."*

"Yes, yes, we should. For B's sake," I sigh and walk over to sit at the end of the couch.

8

My nausea has decreased and my emotions are much less volatile so I do not feel like crying all the time any longer. I feel energetic on most days. However, I have a lot of headaches and dizziness. I also begin to feel this fierce horniness that I subdue by getting into the shower and allowing water to cascade down my body.

"This one you are horny like this," Belema winks and smirks. I roll my eyes.

She sits on my bed, helping me sort my new hair arrivals into *Glam Girl*-branded bags and setting the ring light directly above them. During my first trimester, I barely had time or desire for my business. Even when I did, I would get tired midway and just sleep off, which is why I have been lagging and losing customers. I cried the day I saw that my reel views as well as Instagram followers had decreased. Sobenne promised to help me during the weekend but as each day goes by, the engagements on my Instagram dwindle.

I cried last night on the phone with Belema and she promised to come down and do whatever she could to help.

"I feel like it has to be Tobore but it would be awkward. I don't even know what we are," I say, folding my arms under my breast, my back against the wall.

"I don't support you using that guy, but he is the best bet.

After all, he's the baby daddy." I shrug.

"No one would be more pleased than my parents, especially my mum."

Belema looks up briefly.

"She's still throwing it all in your face?" I nod.

"I think you should tell her how you feel." "Tell her what?" I say, snorting.

"That you know you made a mistake, but their words hurt you emotionally and psychologically. Tell them you are sorry, but the deed has been done and everyone just has to find a way to move forward. Ask them if they would have rather you abort the baby. Tell them that the pressure and the talks get to you. You expect it from everyone outside, but not at home too." I burst into laughter.

"Sounds like something you tell a parent who is not in Nigeria, not the ones I live with. All hell would break lose all over again."

Belema, done setting up the ring light, walks around it.

"I no know again o, sha just try. Make wetin dem dey tell you no too affect you. I know it's hard, it's not as easy as I am making it sound, but just know you have unconditional love that is beyond them. And it's okay to shake off the fear of disappointing them. They are supposed to see you at your worst but still see the best in you, Zim. You are not the only young person who has had sex. Your condom just broke."

I am quiet for a long time after Belema stops talking. I do want my parents to know that their words hurt me, but I am also aware that I cannot compel them to act and speak as though my getting pregnant did not greatly disappoint them. Confronting them with the truth of how much their words hurt me could upset them further and make everything worse.

Belema makes videos of the products set on the bed, shouting in the background. *Better come and buy new hair o, see customers' order. It's not when you hear "'old out" that you will come and start asking o.*

She ends the video, looks at me, and we both burst into laughter.

"The way Instagram vendors lie ehn," she says and shakes her head.

"Na really customers' orders," I guffaw.

I walk over to the bed and gently push the products aside to make space for me to sit. She starts to reset the ring light.

"You have to sit on the chair and wear one of the wigs. I will wear another one so that we can pick a TikTok sound to use, yeah?" I nod, smiling. I watch as she places the chair beside the brand name on the wall so that it will be visible in the background. She sets the ring light and places my phone on the holder. She checks to see if the lighting is good and then she looks at me from behind the ring light and does a thumbs-up.

Her phone rings. She slips it out of her pocket and looks at the caller ID. She shakes her head and puts her phone away. I see her biting her inner cheeks as she continues to steady the ring light.

"Belema."

She shakes her head. "It is nothing."

"Belema."

"Petite, don't worry about it."

"Belema."

She throws her hand in the air. "Fine. I was supposed to do a fitting for a client today at Ikeja. She needs the dress for her wedding. But I told her I was not done with it and would be there by Friday."

"Belema, why would you do that?" I raise my voice a little. "You always finish on time, Belema."

"Yes, I do. I have finished the dress, but I won't get it there until Monday, so forget it."

My eyes trail her as she retrieves the wigs we will wear from the bags. She plays the sound and gestures for me to come to her.

"Was it because of me that you did not go?"

She stares at me with her lips pulled up in a near-sneer, looking very much like a Nigerian mother.

"Who tell you that one now? Abeg, come let us do this video."

I know I am right but Belema would not admit it. She has a habit of leaving what she is doing to be there for me and I wonder how much sacrifice she must have made even without me knowing. I feel the urge to cry but I do not. I stand up and do everything she says as we make TikTok videos together. I sit while she stands so that the high chair can elevate me close to Belema's height with which she set up the ring light.

That night, when Sobenne returns from work, she meets the branded bags at the corner of the room and the set-up Belema and I had used for the videos.

"You did the videos today?" She asks, setting her bag down and then kicking off her brogues. She walks into the bathroom to wash her hands and then comes out drying them on her plaited skirt.

I eye her shoes.

"Belema helped me."

"Oh, that's great. Wow, you're so lucky. Not many of us get lucky with friends," she scoffs. She takes off her shirt and tosses it on the chair.

"I recall one girl that wanted to poison me in Uni. Omo." She sighs and tsks.

I do not have the facility for a full gist, but I prop myself up on my elbow anyway.

"Yeah?" I say.

"Story for another day, baby. I'm hungry." She turns and hurries out of the room.

I sigh and stand up. I pick up her shoes and set them on the rack. I hang her blouse and walk out of the room. As I descend the stairs, I hear the television. I have not sat in the living room in a long time. I know Daddy and Mummy are the ones there because I hear Mummy's angry comment.

"These people, ehn. I'm just ecstatic that people are getting their PVCs. All these wish-walk that undeserving candidates are making will end next year when the votes are cast."

"Amen," Daddy concurs. "After the massacre in 2020, surely no.one wants to dull again. These youths, Gen Z or whatever they call themselves, they are ready for war."

I turn around to return upstairs. It has been so long since I sat in the same room with them to talk, dance, laugh or do any of what we used to do together. These days I feel awkward around them, so I avoid them. Daddy has still not spoken to me, and Mummy's snide comments do not get past me. If we meet in the kitchen, she asks if this is what I have become. If we meet in the living room, she asks if this is what I have become. During morning prayers, she prays that God banishes the spirit of fornication that has taken over me. She anoints me with oil and I feel her index finger pressing hard against my forehead, as though to poke me, as if to say, *Nwatakili a, you disappointed me.*

I understand that I have disappointed and humiliated them. But can I breathe already? The worst part is that Daddy's silence hurts more than Mummy's words.

Something clatters to the ground in the kitchen and I stop midway, wondering what Sobenne has dropped.

"Is it Sobenne that is in the kitchen?" Daddy asks, his voice light.

"Yes. O ya. She is the one."

After a short silence, he speaks again. "Is Zim fine?"

I am so stunned I gasp and tighten my grip on the railings.

"She should be in the room." Mummy's voice comes out muffled like there is something in her mouth. I suspect it is a fruit because I hear her spit out seeds that make light sounds as they fall on the plate.

"Hmm. I hope she is not stressing herself too much."

"She eats well. I check up on her when she is asleep. She is usually so exhausted," Mummy chuckles. "I recall being a lot like that with Jigidem. Feeble, unable to do anything else than sleep like a *tata*."

Daddy laughs. "Yes, I remember. You even slept off during a meeting with my sisters one time, eziokwu, obim, I nearly laughed."

Laughter almost escapes my mouth so I clamp my palm over my mouth.

"I wonder if Sobenne is seeing anyone," Mummy says. "I'm tempted to ask her. Today I saw one of the C.W.O. women from the Ajah branch. Her grandson has just enrolled in my school. She asked about Sobe and wanted to know if she had seen a husband. The audacity."

"We promised not to ask her so she does not feel pressured, Obim. Remember the last time we did, and her mood was bad for weeks?"

"But she is 28. What is she waiting for? If she cannot find a man then we would have to intervene. Look for young men who are ready to wed and are well-to-do. I am still upset by that lady's question. O ka dim n'aru."

Daddy tuts. "Leave her be. Hapu ya, biko. I am sure the right man will come at the appointed time."

They are silent briefly, and then Daddy says, "I miss that abacha mix that Zim makes." I imagine he is rubbing his hand over his bald head and smiling so that the side of his eyes wrinkles. I smile.

"Sobe can make it for you. Should I call her?"

"Mba, I am full. I ate on my way home. I just wanted to munch on something."

"Do I call Zi—"

"Mba!" He booms. I flinch, my hands loosening from the railing.

"Nwayo o. gently."

All the happiness I have been feeling vanishes, replaced by anxiety and nervousness that makes me dizzy. I pull myself down to sit on the stairs.

"She disappointed me, Obim," he says quietly after a short silence. "She is yet to finish her education, yet to find a good-paying job, yet to bring home a *huzzband*," he stomps his feet. "But she is carrying a child in her belly. In my house." He whispers the last part.

"Nkem, the thing gwuru m ike," Mummy concedes. "I don't know how to react. The embarrassment it will bring to me when word gets out. I lead the women at St. Gregory and Umu Ada Agulu looks up to me. What will they say about this family, Nna?" She snaps her fingers, and I picture her crossing her legs and leaning back into the couch. "O di outrageous. Even bothersome is the fact that the boy has refused to marry her." I feel a tear fall.

"She will have to stop going to church with us. Even the wedding on Saturday, she cannot go," Mummy continues. "It is too embarrassing. The utter shame."

"And that Tobore boy does not seem forthcoming. We don't even see him in this house. If not the father of the child, what suitor would come, really, Obim? I am so afraid of what being unmarried and being a mother might do to Zim. This is not how I envisioned her life." Daddy hisses.

"It is an outrageous situation, Nna. One that we must curtail. We promised to secure bright futures for these children, but look at our last born, ruining herself before her life begins to fall in place.

The thing gwuru m ike. Emotionally, I am discombobulated."

Tears cascade down my face. The heaviness that grips me shakes me alert. I need to get out of here. I need to be away from this house. I wish I never got pregnant. I wish Nelson had not been at home that day. I wish Tobore had agreed to marry me. I wish I would just have a miscarriage. I clamp my hand over my mouth to keep my sobs quiet. I look up to the top of the stairs and wonder if it is safe to let myself fall so that this baby may die but I would live.

I stand up and walk out of the house quietly. In the compound, I call Belema, but she does not answer. So, I call Tobore.

"Sissy, sissy, why are you crying? Is everything alright?" He asks.

"I am tired, Tobore. I am tired."

He is silent for a while. "Where are you? Are you home?"

"Yes. But I am so tired. Why am I even pregnant? Why did I not abort this baby so I can have peace of mind? I am so fucking tired of all the judgements! To abort, problem. To keep the child, problem. What exactly does the world fucking want!"

In a voice so tranquil, he says. "Where are you, Sissy? Let me come to you."

It is already dark when Tobore arrives in an Uber. He wears orange shorts and a black shirt and approaches me carrying a white nylon bag. I am standing outside when I see him. My tears have dried up but the pain is not gone. When he reaches me, he embraces me. I press my body into him, close my eyes and inhale his smell. I rest my head on his shoulder and allow him to rub my back, kiss my ear, and whisper to me. What is it about hugging him that calms me?

"Take a walk with me?" His voice is husky and he gazes at me intensely so I nod. We hold hands and begin to walk. He moves to my left side to walk between me and the cars driving past us.

"What is it, Sissy? What is making you so sad?"

I shrug and kick a pebble out of my way. "I am tired. Everywhere I turn, someone is judging me. At the hospital, at home, on the internet."

He squeezes my hand. "I"m sorry you have to go through all of this, Sissy. I just need your permission to rough up anyone who has been making you feel this way. You know, just give them small beating."

I chuckle.

"I wish there was something I could do."

There was, I want to scream. *There fucking was. You should have agreed to marry me. You should have taken me away from that house and put a ring on my finger so that I do not have to bear these insults.*

The night breeze kisses my skin and I shiver. With Tobore here, I wonder a lot of things. I wonder what we are doing. What the plan for the baby is. If I should even have this baby at all. Maybe I would throw myself down the staircase after all. Might be a better option than all this pain. Maybe they would get over the baby dying rather than me carrying a swollen belly and disgracing them.

Tobore rubs his thumb against the back of my palm, and warmth fills me. I sigh.

"What do we want? I feel like we have never discussed this pregnancy and life beyond it," he says suddenly and looks at me. He licks his lips. I am distracted, so I swallow and look away.

We approach the estate park and he dusts the chair before I sit and settles beside me.

"Ehen, Asa," he begins in a feigned Igbo accent. "Do you want bread?"

I look at him, and then at the nylon bag he is holding. I laugh.

I collect the bag from him and place it on my thigh.

"Till now, I am yet to accept that I want this baby," I confess. "I am yet to admit that this baby is coming. I'm still so consumed by the fact that there is so much judgment directed at me."

"That's understandable, honestly. And I fear it's taking a toll on your mental health." He bites his lip.

I lean towards him when I begin to feel the breeze against my bare arms.

"Maybe," I whisper.

He clears his throat. "I honestly would want you to spend some more time with me." His left arm reaches across to my left shoulder, where goosebumps have sprouted as the cold hits. His big fingers rub against them, going up, down, up, down, until my entire body starts to shiver. But not from cold.

The air around me heats up, my stomach twists and my right leg presses against his left one. I close my eyes as a surge passes through my body. I want his hand, his lips—anything. Everything.

I suddenly feel his breath against my neck, hot and gratifying.

"Tobore," I whisper.

He pulls away and clears his throat.

"Sorry, sorry." He stands up rapidly, looks at the sky and whistles dramatically. "It's dark, mehn. How did we miss that, ehn?"

My body is still shaken from what had just happened. His eyes refuse to meet mine even though I seek them. And when they finally settle on me, he has a longing look in them.

I lean back against the backrest, panting.

"Fuck," I mutter.

He licks his lips and shakes his head. I close my eyes. I want to say something, anything to keep myself from asking if we can kiss, do a hanky-panky. Anything.

"What are the things that set you off and make you feel the way you did when you called me? What are the things that hurt you?" he asks.

The faraway look has left his eyes.

"When people ask who the father is. When people look at my finger and do not see a ring. When my parents see me as a disappointment." I shrug and look away, then back at him.

"Everything, really."

"What do you want to do, Zim? What do you really want?" His voice is rasp and intense and I do not know what to make of it. "I want to stop feeling this way: I feel like I don't want this baby, that I'm not ready to have a baby, but I also don't want to disappoint my family," I say. Then I laugh. What an irony. It is the people who hurt me that I do not want to disappoint. It is the people who have caused my greatest pain that I carry this child for.

"So what choices are we making?" He draws nearer to me and squats so that our eyes are in closer proximity, but he does not hold me.

"I want to feel all the love I felt before this pregnancy. I want to be at peace again."

"If you want to keep this baby," he says, looking at my belly, "do it for you, otherwise you'll end up resenting him or her and it would take a toll on your life, Sissy. On his or her life, and even mine."

I stare at his eyes, his lips, his hairline, his eyebrows. I let my eyes trace the curves on his face. I look at him and somehow, I see hope. I see how I can want to keep the baby, make my family proud, and have some of that love I had before this pregnancy back. I see how there can be light in every way, I see how Tobore can make all of this better, so I lean in and my lips hover over his, our breathings rough, close, hot.

"Why did you stand up?" I mutter, looking at his lips, how plump they are.

"Zim, I don't want us to do something you might regret."

"Is this about the pregnancy?" My hand reaches out to touch his face.

"All of it. Including when I asked you out and you refused, and I just wanted to give you space. I-I don't think you really like me." His gaze is soft and sad.

"I don't want space," I whisper curtly. We're so close now that our lips touch each other.

"Are you sure, Zim? I have held myself for a very long time. If we do this now, it could ruin everything," he says and grunts, closing his eyes.

"Kiss me, Tobore. Please."

He covers my lips with his, his tongue, hot and needy, dancing against it. He tastes of banana bread.

I wrap my arms around his shoulders and sink into the kiss, allowing his lips to move against mine. I feel my body's resolve melting. There is a light in my brain. This is the first step to making it all better.

9

They say you cannot force a man to do something he does not want to. There is a decision power generally bestowed upon men. During the talking stage, even in *situationships*, we are accustomed to waiting for the man to make the decisive move that would make the relationship official. So, we hang around and wait anxiously, an anxiety that sometimes grows into fury.

When the fuck will he ask?

Well, you can nudge him to do what needs to be done for both of you. Waiting can be frustrating, so push things, and manipulate things, so that they play out in your favour. This is what I plan to do with Tobore because he is offering me nothing and I want something.

After that kiss, our situationship has bloomed. But I can tell that he has become cautious. He sends me messages in the mornings and we converse so frequently now it feels like we are jobless teenagers. Our phone calls last longer and he is more expressive.

Nonetheless, I can tell that he has become cautious.

"I miss frenching you," he said one night on the phone.

I guffawed while trying to raise my legs against the wall. Sobenne poked her head out of the bathroom door and glared at me.

"You are making noise, Baby. I'm trying to sing along to Mercy Chinwo."

I muttered a sorry and the call continued.

He begins to visit every day. At first, he would call me to come outside, and we would take a stroll and he would kiss me senselessly at the park. But since I want something more, I need to set things in proper motion.

I was reluctant to tell Belema about this new development because I know what her reaction would be. I tell her now during an evening phone call.

"You do wetin?" She exclaims.

"We kissed and all. Maybe we can explore something serious from here."

Belema laughs mockingly and I roll my eyes.

"Zimife! Are you sure you like this guy? Because you did not tell me you like him o. And now you have kissed and are 'exploring' something serious from here," she says, mimicking me.

"I don't like this your reaction, abeg. What's wrong with kissing and wanting to be happy?"

"I know you're hurt by how your parents have handled this whole situation, but you shouldn't use Tobore to feel better. You don't need him by your side to feel important, especially if your feelings for him are still uncertain."

I am annoyed because I know it is so convenient for her to say and visualise in her head. She is not the one who has had to endure all I have been enduring. The other day, Mummy had visitors over. She asked me to go to my room and remain there and asked Sobenne to bring me whatever I needed that was not in the room. Her face, how agitated she was as she spoke, made me want to hide away forever.

With Tobore, it can all be better.

"You're not the one who is pregnant, Belema. You're not the one facing all this," I lash out.

She sighs.

"No do wetin go push person commot for your side, my guy. Sometimes, selfish actions like this can cost you the best people. Tobore is a good one."

"I know, which is why I want him to stay in my life."

The call with Belema upset me more than I would have liked. I just wish she could see things through my eyes and see just how much I need her support on this one.

Tobore tells me that he would visit in the evening with my favourite banana bread and some other goodies. On my way down the stairs, I deliberately miss a step on the staircase. The intent is not to hurt myself, but I nearly fall face flat. My scream is piercing and Daddy, the only one at home, rushes out of the living room. "Zimife," He calls, holding me by my waist so that I lean against him. My eyes widen, because I have not been this physically close to him in a long time. I swallow and stare down at my leg.

It does not hurt so much. However, I scream with every step and feign a limp.

"You should be more careful," Daddy scolds, as he guides me to the living room.

After I sit on the couch, Daddy rushes to the kitchen. My phone rings just as Daddy comes out with some ice. It is Tobore.

"Hello," I say, my voice shaking more than it should.

"Are you alright? You don't sound good."

"I sprained my ankle," I mutter. Daddy returns with an ice pack and sits beside me. He places the ice on my ankle and I yell.

He mutters an apology in Igbo.

"Ah! Is it bad? Can you walk?" Tobore asks.

"If you're here, you can just come inside," I say into the phone and scream again.

Daddy pauses and glares at me.

"I barely touched it. Who are you inviting into the house at this time?"

"Tobore," I say, my voice edgy. Daddy also has to believe that I am badly hurt. He rubs my knee, mutters another apology and presses the ice gently on my ankle. Tobore knocks and comes into the house.

I lean back into the chair and close my eyes as if in serious pain.

"Ahan, Tobore?" Daddy feigns surprise at seeing him and I almost giggle.

Tobore walks into the living room looking perplexed. He is holding white nylon bags and I assume they are filled with the things I said I wanted: ice cream, banana bread, burnt chicken, and nail polish—because I like the smell. He places them on the centre table. He is wearing a t-shirt that hugs his biceps over a pair of jeans.

"Tobore," I call out weakly and offer a feeble smile. My eyes dart to the nylon and I sigh. "Oh, you got everything. Thank you so much."

Tobore reaches out to shake Daddy while looking at me.

"Please, sit," Daddy says, then smiles weakly. "We are the only ones at home, Sobe would have brought something for you."

"No," Tobore shakes his head as he sits adjacent to me. "It is alright, sir. I just came to see Zim. Came to check how she's doing." Daddy nods and rubs my ankle gently.

"It is just a little sprain. She will be fine."

I want the conversation between them to keep going. I want Tobore to say something that insinuates that we are a thing, that we are together. I do not care how silly it might sound; I just want the idea to be thrown into the open.

"Do you want to stroll, Tobore? We can just—"

"No," he says sharply and shakes his head. "You need to stay put, Sissy. We can talk here; it's no worries."

I nod, smiling. "How's work?"

"Very fine, thanks." He grins. I can tell he is happier about work these days. All his plans are falling into place, and at night when he is not talking to me, he listens to audiobooks of Napoleon Hill, Earl Nightingale, and the like because he believes their teachings will influence his mindset and actions positively.

"Good to hear," I say. Daddy looks at us and looks away.

"Uh, Toby, what is it you said you do?" Daddy asks.

I nearly burst into laughter.

"Daddy, where did you hear Toby from again?" Daddy grins.

"Is it not Tobo-re? The short form should be Toby now."

I burst out laughing. Daddy chuckles and pushes at my feet jocosely.

"You cannot correct me without mocking me, ehn, Zim of Africa."

It has been so long since I heard him call me that, since he spoke to me directly, and I feel such delight. We are even laughing together.

"Daddy, Daddy," I say.

He smiles as he faces Tobore.

"Sorry if I miscalled your name. But people who bear that name, the short form is usually Toby, abi?"

"It is Tobore, Efetobore. It means 'Wealth has now been achieved.'"

"Oh, ehen... That is really nice. Wonderful name. I will learn the pronunciation. So Tob...ore. What is the surname you told me that other time?"

"Edewor."

"Wonderful. Tobore, wadoo."

Tobore laughs, looking from Daddy to me. I am surprised that Daddy is greeting him in Urhobo. It means that he wants Tobore to feel comfortable in this house. I smile.

"Good to have you here again," Daddy says.

Tobore nods. He looks meek, like one who could not have said, "Let me French you, Sissy" or moan against my lips. I swallow. Maybe Belema is right. I should just tell Tobore that I am horny.

"So, what do you do again? I remember you were explaining it to her elder brother at the hospital that day but I was not paying much attention." Daddy relaxes on the couch, one hand on my feet.

I look at Tobore. It seems the question has made him uncomfortable. I remember Tobore telling me he did not like discussing the goals he had yet to accomplish last year right before he told me about his fintech startup. I feel terrible that he has been put in this position now, but this is necessary to set everything in motion as I want. Daddy has to see that he is responsible and that he can be a good man for me. He needs to see that the father of this child I am carrying is going to do well.

"I own a fintech company, sir. It is a company that uses new technology to aid the delivery of financial services. There is a lot more to that, but I would not want to bore you with the little details."

Daddy nods. I see a crinkle at the corner of his eyes and I know he is somewhat pleased.

"That is very good. Consistency is the key to success in any business. And God willing, you will achieve everything you want to." "Thank you, sir," Tobore says, smiling. My heart flutters.

"So, how has it been starting up?" Daddy goes on.

And the conversation blooms from there, and satisfaction dances within me. Tobore quickly becomes bolder in the conversation because Daddy is a good listener and always has something good to say in return and advice to offer.

As I watch Tobore talk to Daddy, seated upright, shoulders squared, brows furrowed, lips moving with assurance and confidence in what he says, heat surges through me. There is a lot more he can do with those lips than just talking. If I were light skinned, my cheeks would have been red from blushing. But I shield my smile with my palm, pretending to yawn over and over again when, truly, I want to cuddle with him. I want to wrap my hands around Tobore and kiss him. I want him to rub my back and my feet. I want him to do all of those things I see in the movies, but I know that it cannot happen here.

When mummy and Sobenne return home, they are surprised to see Tobore. Mummy just greets Tobore and goes upstairs to change, while Sobenne lingers around enough to exchange glances with me, glances that ask, "Still a situationship?"

Tobore leaves late, but before he does, he takes my hand in his and rubs his thumb against the back of my palm. I wish he could lean in to peck me.

We grow closer, Tobore and I. On our hospital visits, he holds my hand as we wait in the reception and walk to Dr Isioma's office. Even when he makes a call, he holds me to him, rubbing my hand, keeping me close as though to show that I am his, as though afraid that I might vanish. I like it. The judgmental receptionist with the strange stare watches us, sometimes I catch her smiling, and sometimes she shakes her head. But I do not care anymore.

As the weeks go by, I become hornier, increasingly seeking sex. On one of the visits, I ask Dr Isioma if it is alright to have sex during pregnancy. She says that it is very much alright, and then she wriggles her brows. It is on this visit that Nelson speaks to me. He comes into Dr Isioma's office in the middle of my prenatal ultrasound, my gaze switching from being tender to her and being blank to him.

"Zimife."

"Jigidem."

He folds his hand across his chest and grunts. "How have you been?"

"This is a private session, Pharm. Ike-Steven," Dr. Isioma says, looking at the monitor briefly before jotting down on the large notepad.

Nelson clears his throat.

"You will forgive me for coming in here like this. I just wanted to check on my sister. See how things are going before I head to lunch."

Dr. Isioma moves the stethoscope around my abdomen and I see that she is trying to suppress a smile.

"Oh, lunch," she says.

Tobore squeezes my hand. I want to yelp, but I glare at him instead. He raises an eyebrow, smirking. Then his eyes dart rapidly between the doctor and my brother before settling back on me. We both burst into laughter so suddenly that Dr Isioma flinches.

"There is a heartbeat, I can hear it."

Nelson's eyes widen and his brows ridge. "There is?"

Tobore shifts closer, his eyes wide as he stares at the monitor. I tilt my head a bit to see the black-and-white image undulating on the screen. I see the tiny form in the image and feel such joy. I giggle. I feel Tobore's hand holding mine. The air is pacific. For the first time since I found out about this pregnancy, I see a picture of myself carrying a child in my arms. I imagine Tobore by my side, cooing from behind my ears. I imagine a cot, then I see Daddy dancing, Belema holding a handmade blanket, Sobenne making the baby food, Mummy setting baby books on a shelf and Nelson standing by the door, arms across his chest, a smile on his face.

Dr Isioma gestures to us and we all focus to listen to the heartbeat. Nelson ambles over to listen as well. The excitement from everyone, the smile from Nelson, the clap from Tobore, the nod from Dr Isioma when she says, "Healthy baby, Zim. Your baby is healthy."

This is what I crave, to be surrounded by all this love on this journey.

10

I watch water swirl in the sink until it bubbles and disappears down the drain. I turn on the tap again and watch the same thing play out. It is a Saturday afternoon. The weather is hot. I have this strong desire to take off my large t-shirt and walk around in only my biker shorts. I am standing in Tobore's kitchen, looking out the window. My eyes settle on the vines atop the grey fence. They look as though they are sneaking about spying, with their spiky stems and small leaves growing in odd places. If one stares for too long, it begins to look like a snake.

"What are you thinking about, Sissy?"

I yelp, bumping my belly lightly against the sink. Tobore hisses and rushes to my side.

"I am so sorry. Are you alright? Does it hurt?" He looks frantic. His hand is on my belly, his head bent down, turning to check my belly from different sides. It is so pleasing to watch and I proceed to act out a scene from a Nollywood movie I once saw.

"Here," I whisper, patting my lips, waiting for him to lift his eyes.

Tobore stands upright. His creased brows remain that way until his eyes follow my finger. His face softens and his shoulder droops a little. He leans in, bending slightly, and parts his plump lips. I wrap my arms around his neck as his lips wrap themselves over and into mine. I allow him to do with me as he pleases.

My family is attending a wedding. They have had a wedding to attend for the past few consecutive Saturdays. With my protruding belly visible in all my dresses, my nose wider and my feet swollen, it is a dead giveaway. Mummy—now more cordial with me with comments like, "You look good in pregnancy, I like the cheeks it has given you, but that nose must be a punishment"— would never allow me to disgrace her in public. Besides, I am too embarrassed to attend such events anyway. The people we know who see me would ask when palm wine was brought to my house and they were not told; some would ask directly if the pregnancy is out of wedlock.

So, I did not even attempt to go, and no one bothered to ask. I asked Tobore if he was busy, and that if he was not, would he mind keeping me company? When I said I did not mind coming to his place, he came to pick me up.

His hands descend to my buttocks, and he squeezes them. His lips continue to ravish me, his tongue probing inside my mouth.

This is a good time to tell him about my horniness. I have avoided it for weeks, only kissing and cuddling.

I know what Tobore likes. Especially when the moment is heated up like this.

"Tobore," I moan. "I want D."

He rears his head backwards, still holding me. "You cannot say the word with your full chest?" "Tobore!" I cry out, giggling.

He laughs. "Come on, Sissy, you're a big girl now, you should be able to say it."

I let go of him, feeling abashed. With pouted lips and eyes cast to the ground, I slip out of his hold and stomp my way to the living room. Tobore follows me. His attempts to stifle his laughter are futile. I sit on the couch and lean into the armrest. Tobore plumps down on the same couch. He raises my feet onto his thigh and looks at me sideways. One side of his lips is pulled up, and I just know that he is being mischievous.

He rubs my sole sensually.

"I want that too," he says calmly. "But I don't want you to get hurt."

"There are good positions we can try," I say. I clear my throat and close my eyes, enjoying the foot massage.

He inhales rapidly and goes on. "We would have to ask your doctor."

"But she already told me it's safe. I asked."

He looks surprised. "How long have you been thinking about this?"

"Long," I smirk.

Tobore shakes his head and laughs. He pats my sole and grins. "Come on, let's do some mummy and daddy duty."

I am unable to hold myself from laughing. I feel giddy inside. I stand up immediately and so does Tobore. He holds my waist as we walk into his bedroom.

The sex is wonderful but somewhat uncomfortable. We struggle to find positions that ensure he is fully hitting it. I try to ride him but bouncing my stomach up and down scares me. What if this deforms the baby? We finally settle on spooning: he behind me, I in front; my legs parted to accommodate his largeness. My body heats up. I grip the blue sheets and moan. Sometimes I hear myself scream. Tobore thrusts with such precision. He stops himself severally from squeezing my breast because I said they ache. He places his hand on my chest and caresses my breasts lightly, and my neck. He caresses me anywhere.

Pleasure spikes. I can tell from the way he grunts, the nasty words he whispers and the way he hastens his thrusts, that he is approaching his climax. And this is when it happens. The cramps.

A sudden, sharp twist in my abdomen.

"Ah," I scream, tapping Tobore.

He slows down and then stills. I tap him again, my eyes closed.

"Jesus, my stomach. Jesus."

Tobore slips out of me and kneels before me. "Hey, Sissy, are you alright?"

I shake my head. "Call Dr Isioma, please. Ah!" The tightening in my abdomen increases, and I feel stiff. My stomach feels as though something is being squeezed like wet laundry.

Dr Isioma answers on the third ring.

"Hello, good afternoon."

"Good afternoon, Doc," Tobore starts. He goes on to tell her that I am in pain. It is the first time that I have been in pain around Tobore. Maybe that is why the way he acts is all new to me. He is touching my belly and rubbing it as he speaks to Dr Isioma. His brows are deeply furrowed. I can hear his voice shaking slightly; I can see his eyeballs bouncing. This is the way he panics. Even in his panic, he still tries to be calm.

"She said does it feel like cramps?" He whispers to me.

I nod. He places the call on speakerphone.

"It will pass, just stay calm. Were you doing anything strenuous? Exercise or ..." Dr Isioma stretches the 'or' and lingers.

Tobore and I look at each other. The mischievous glint in his eyes is highlighted by his smile.

"Something like that," he says with a grin.

Dr Isioma laughs. Then she clears her throat almost immediately.

"Well, if you do wish to continue, bear in mind that the cramps will as well. It is called Braxton Hicks and poses no danger." Just as she says this, the cramping reduces.

"Alright, Doc. Thank you."

"Have a good day. And please call again if anything else happens."

"Sure will," Tobore says and hangs up.

"The pain has reduced," I say.

He hops off the bed and pulls on a pair of shorts. Then he turns to me.

"No more, abeg. I don't want to hurt you or the baby."

I lay on my side now, my elbow plopped on a pillow, my breasts leaning sideways, one leg over the other. Tobore licks his lips as he stares at me.

"The way you are looking at me is not helpful."

"What? What did I do?"

"Oh, come on, Sissy," he groans and slides a hand into his pocket. He climbs the bed and crawls towards me. He leans in and presses his lips against mine. His hand wraps my waist and then he settles beside me.

"You are so sexy, Sissy."

I flick my tongue on his nose. "With my wide nose?"

He guffaws. "With your wide nose, baby."

He rests his head on my chest, his hand still on my waist. "Do you think the baby will be a girl?"

I pause and wonder. I have never really thought about it. A girl or a boy. What does it matter?

"I don't know. I don't think I ever really thought about it."

He draws circles on my waist with his finger. "I have. She will have three names. One Igbo, one English, one Urhobo."

"That would be nice."

He looks up at me. "Hm hmm." He plants a kiss on my lips.

"She will look like you. Big nose—" he kisses my nose, "Nice bow-shaped lips—" he kisses my lips, "Dark skin—" he kisses my cheek.

My palms are sweaty. I am distracted so I find the kisses intrusive. What if it is a girl or a boy? How does one raise either gender? I stare at the wall, my eyes lingering on the black-andwhite painting of Tobore hung on it. Surely, he would create a space here for the baby to stay. Because for the first year of the baby's life, I would be in school. Mummy works, Daddy does as well, and so does Sobenne. Who would have time to take care of the baby? Maybe Tobore would hire a nanny, so they can care for the baby until I get back.

I rub my palms against the sheets. Tobore begins to suck my breasts. His tongue against it is tender, hot, and pleasing. It is at this moment that I am drawn out of my thoughts. He grabs my waist and guides my head to rest on his chest. I close my eyes and inhale his smell.

Later, Tobore orders takeout and we eat, watch movies, and banter until I sleep off. I wake up with my head on Tobore's thigh. I feel rice in my mouth. My shoulders sag as I groan. This has been happening often: I wake up and feel already-swallowed food in my mouth. Dr Isioma said it is normal, but it is discomforting whenever it happens. I glance at Tobore. His left arm is across his face. There is a power outage, so the television has turned off and the room is hot.

I check the time on my phone. It is past six. I stand up slowly and walk to the bathroom in his bedroom. I wash my hands, squeeze toothpaste on a finger and wash my mouth with it.

When I return to the living room. I tap Tobore's thigh as I settle beside him. He wakes up slowly. His eyes flutter open and he stares at me.

"Hey, sissy."

"I have to go home, baby," I say and pout.

He checks the time on his phone and frowns.

"Yeah, we should take you home."

When the car halts in front of my house, Tobore leans in and kisses me on my lips.

"I really liked how today went."

"Me too," I admit. "I liked it a lot." I smile.

He smiles back and nods, then licks his lips.

"I was thinking. We need to start getting baby things. We can buy neutral colours until we do the next scan."

I frown and lean into the car seat. I do not think I want to know the gender of the baby yet, not until he or she is born. I feel that knowing the baby's gender now diminishes the thrill when the baby eventually slides out of me.

"I don't think I want to know yet."

"Why?" Tobore, taken aback, asks.

I shrug.

"I don't know." I shrug again.

"Is it necessary?"

He nods. "Yes. It is. We need to know what gender we're buying things for, and know how to prepare properly."

"No, I don't want to know."

"Wahala." He tsks. "So, if we are buying things now, the ones that are colour-specific, what colours do we buy?"

"Neutral colours, like you said." "That will make planning disorganised." He sounds offended.

The truth is, with this baby, I have barely sat to think a lot of these things through. And it is a gradual process for me. This is going to be my first child. I do not want to be rushed into decisionmaking. What if the scan is wrong and we buy all the wrong things because the baby ends up being born as a different gender?

"See, I have seen stuff on Instagram, where the baby is born and then it is not what was expected. They bought everything and it ended up being a waste."

Tobore shakes his head. "It is not the same for everyone, and I doubt it would be the same for us."

"What if we buy things for a girl, then we give birth to a boy and then—"

Tobore shakes his head. "You know what?" Tobore cuts in, "Let's not argue about this. We would shop neutral." He shakes his head.

I nod. After the baby is born then we can shop according to gender. I alight from the car, still a bit annoyed that he even argued with me in the first place. I mean, I am the one carrying the baby and facing all the backlash that comes with it. Even today, during sex, my body rebelled against me. I do not like that he made it seem as though my idea was ludicrous. Telling me "'That will make planning disorganised". Really?

I hear the door jam and footsteps approach me. I turn around. Tobore raises his hands in the air in surrender.

"Hey, we might not agree on the same things, but we have to at least meet halfway at some point and understand where each person is coming from. I did get your point, Sissy."

He approaches me gradually until he is holding me and rubbing my forearm.

"Sissy."

"You sounded like I was not making any sense."

He closes his eyes. "You were. I just was not agreeing, Sissy. I'm sorry."

I pucker up my lips. He leans down and presses his against mine. "Apology accepted, my baby."

"Goodnight." He kisses me chastely.

I turn away from him. And just before I walk away, he taps my ass, causing me to yelp from the shock, while holding my bum and running inside.

Even as I walk past the threshold, I feel the pleasing sting of his hand against my ass.

11

The only pictures I have from this period are the ones Belema took of me when we made TikTok videos for my business. At month seven, my stomach is the size of a large watermelon, and I feel gravid. Sobe says I now walk like an old woman, my legs flying at opposite directions, in addition to my swollen feet. Sobenne bursts into laughter each time she sees me walking.

I am in a photo studio. Belema, Sobenne and Tobore stand behind the cameraman and watch as shots are taken. Belema was having none of it when I said I was too tired to take a picture. She had to get Sobenne involved and Sobe offered to drive us to the studio in Mummy's car.

I am wearing a yellow satin two-piece that Belema made for me specially for this shoot. The cloth makes me feel celestial. The hem of the skirt covers my legs and the blouse is a sleeveless crop top that reveals my stomach. I hold my belly in my hands in most of the poses. In others, I strike random poses, including one where I bare my teeth at Tobore, who does not like pictures, but he agrees to take only two with me. In those, he pleads that we make eye contact because he is camera-shy. Belema and Sobenne take a few with me, and the photographer promises to send them to Belema, who has offered to pay for all of them.

"Because, really, how you go get this fine belle and you no get picture," she says after the shoot.

Sobenne and Tobore have walked ahead of us. Tobore is looking at his phone and Sobenne is making an angry call. Belema and I walk together, holding hands. Her hands are soft and comfortable to hold.

"How was it?" she flicks her brows, looking at Tobore. That night, after the sex, I texted Belema to squeal, and to reveal that pregnancy sex was not so bad. But Belema did not want to hear about it over the phone, and she never had enough time to see me. Between running around Lagos to do fittings, sewing, helping me post on my Instagram, sewing me a surprise dress and planning this photoshoot, she had very little time to come down to Sangotedo.

"It was fine, I really liked it," I bit my lips. "He really hit it and it was going so well, ugh. Just contractions that spoilt it."

"Aww," she pouts. "Look at your face. Look how happy you are. Na this expression confam say our brother do you well." She elbows me lightly. "I am happy that you are happy."

I squeeze her hand and smile. We are in the parking lot of the complex where the photo studio is located, laughing, gossiping in hush tones, and making silly sounds.

"How's Ned? How are you guys?" I ask. Since the last time I stumbled on Ned at her home, I have not seen or heard of him.

"Ned is good. He'll finally be done with NYSC next month and have my time properly," she says, grinning. Her cheeks are so red and I chuckle.

"But yeah, that's it. And we've been talking a lot about the future. Omo, I just want them to call off this strike—"

"Hey, hey, not yet," I interject, pointing to my stomach. "Let me born first."

Belema shakes her head. "Okay, let them hold off a bit until you can give birth to my godchild."

"Good girl." We high five, and the clap calls the attention of Sobenne and Tobore.

Tobore stops walking, waiting for me to catch up. When I draw nearer, I see that his mood has soured. I let go of Belema to meet him. He forces a smile when I reach him, then he bends to kiss my nose.

"I have to run, Sissy. I'll see you later." He glances at his phone briefly. "And some things have been sent to your house. The baby cot, a trolley and the breast pumps. Exactly the ones we ordered yesterday. Check them out and tell me if you like them. If you don't, we can always return them."

"Thank you, my baby," I squeal, then I lean in to kiss him. He shakes his head, still smiling. Then he waves at Sobenne and Belema. He walks to his car and only after he has driven away do I remember that I forgot to ask him if he is alright.

Everything we ordered is just how I wanted it. Daddy and Sobenne clear out Sobe's old room, while mummy cooks in the kitchen. Nelson offers to come with a painter the following day to paint the room before we set everything up. When everyone returns from church, we all sit downstairs in the dining room and have brunch together. It has been long since we did this and my face is frozen in a smile. Everyone has come to terms with my pregnancy. Mummy and Daddy now gossip more about how Tobore and I would eventually get married in the future; Sobenne seems distracted, and I wonder what is bothering her; and Nelson seems less angry.

"So, I am seeing someone," he says suddenly after the meal, while he flosses his teeth.

Mummy, who sits beside him, turns to him, her lips parted. "Eziokwu? Do you speak the truth, Nnam?"

Nelson relaxes in the chair and laughs robustly. He nods. "Yes. I wanted to bring her to the dinner months ago, but that dinner never took place. The one—"

"At Eko hotel," I cut in. I close my eyes and sigh deeply.

Nelson must have taken the day off then to prepare for this announcement. He must have been so nervous that day that he went for a run before he came back and met me.

"Yes," he says casually. "That one."

I can bet that I know who the woman is whom he wants to introduce to us. I suppress my giggle when he begins to talk about her.

"Uhm, she is a doctor at the hospital where I work—" "I knew it!" I blurt out, pointing at him and laughing.

"Shut up," Nelson says and glares at me. I suppress my laughter and nod. He can have the floor and prance to victory. It is all his.

"I can bring her over to the house next weekend."

"Please do," Mummy says. Her eyes are wide and her grin is so broad I imagine that her cheeks would soon start to ache.

Daddy has been quiet, but his smile says a lot. Sobenne also has a similar smile. Everyone is thrilled.

The painter comes downstairs just then, his clothes stained with blue paint. He stands at the threshold, raising the near-empty paint bucket.

"I don paint am finish." He smells of fresh paint. Nelson looks up at him.

"Send me the total money, Wasiu. I go do transfer for you." Nelson looks up at him. Wasiu nods. Sobenne shows him the way out. Everyone resumes celebrating that Nelson is seeing someone.

Later, in the kitchen, I catch Sobenne staring at the pot on the fire like someone lost in a trance.

Tobore grows increasingly distant in the days that follow. Our night walks are reduced. He stops calling as often as he used to and has become very forgetful. He spends a lot of his time on his phone texting, making calls, and sending voice notes I can tell are angry-toned from the way his facial muscles flex from a distance. On our next hospital visit, he does not bring me banana bread as he usually does, and he does not hold my hand as we stand from the waiting area to walk into Dr Isioma's office. The only time he makes an input during the checkup is towards the end of our visit when he asks Dr Isioma questions I had not even thought about.

"When can we feel the baby kick?" He asks.

"It's her first pregnancy, so anytime from—" she tilts her head to one side and back, "25 weeks."

"What would that feel like? Would she know it's kicking? Or would it just feel like cramps?" He asks pointedly, his phone beeping irritably.

Dr Isioma looks at me and smiles.

"She should be able to tell it's a kick. Don't worry."

My palms become sweaty. The baby would start kicking soon. I force a smile as I look from Tobore to Dr Isioma and back, wondering what kind of pain the kicking might inflict. I stare down at my stomach and stare at the floral print of the Ankara blouse.

Tobore gets distracted again. I hear the clicks of his phone's keypad, tapping away like legwork on a tiled floor. I wonder why he cannot hold everything off till we leave the hospital.

In the car, I ask him what the problem is but he shrugs it off and says it is nothing. It is a minor issue at work that he needs to fix. But I am not certain the issue is minor. It affects the attention he gives me. It affected us at the hospital when, for instance, the receptionist was on duty and she looked at our unlinked hands, judging. Whatever is bothering him is eating into our lives and it is disturbing me.

He drops me at home and kisses me briefly. No tease, no intense gaze, nothing. I ask him again if he is fine and he says he is.

At night I am unable to sleep. I toss and turn, stare at the ceiling and, at a point, I watch Sobenne's unmoving form. Her back is to me, and I realise that we have barely spoken in the past few days. She had seemed so busy.

I pick up my phone. It is 11:30. I open WhatsApp, ignore all the hair request messages and open Tobore's chat. I see that he is online. I send a text.

Hey baby.

His online status disappears, but my message has two grey ticks. I wait for the ticks to turn blue, but it does not happen. I decide to call him. He answers on the first ring. His voice is rasp, and tired.

"Hey, I saw that you were online," I whisper. "Yeah, a while ago. I am about to sleep now."

I sigh. "I can't sleep. I keep tossing."

"Sorry, sissy," he mutters. "Try to get some sleep, or should I send you some music that may help you sleep?"

"Not one of those rap songs you listen to o."

He chuckles. "I will send you something. Goodnight."

But I want to talk more. He has, in the past, stayed on the phone with me until I started to feel sleepy. How come he wants to leave me now?

"Um, okay."

The call ends. I stare at my screen, wondering what is going on. Everything was perfect, everything was going well. What is the problem now?

"Ha. Na wa o," I mutter, dropping my phone on the nightstand.

"You good?" Sobenne asks. I am startled. I turn to face her.

Her elbow is plopped on the pillow and she looks at me expectantly.

"Tobore has been acting strange. Distant."

"Have you asked him what the problem is?"

I nod. "Many times. And he keeps saying nothing is wrong. Is that what guys do when they don't like you anymore? I know Tobore is soft-hearted. Maybe he wants to withdraw so I can call him out."

Sobenne shakes her head. "Or maybe it's not about you, Baby. It might be about something else going on in his life and he is just not ready to talk about it. You should just relax, show your support and allow him to come to you when he's ready."

I find her words comforting and I hold on to them for a while, but things worsen with Tobore to the point where I become utterly irritated. I begin to expect him to disappoint me. He forgets hospital visits, saying he mixed the dates up in his schedule and this made us late for appointments. I mean, he works from home.

All his fintech company thing happens at home. He does his cryptocurrency and online product selling from the comfort of his bedroom. So, what does he mean he mixed it up?

It becomes glaring to me that something is off and it is about me.

"You forgot, Tobore? How could you forget?"

His hair is unkempt. His beard has not been trimmed in longer than usual and there are circles beneath his eyes.

"You look tired. Did you not sleep? You worked overnight and just forgot that we have this appointment?"

Even when the appointment is over my anger lingers like a stench from a soak-away. I know how hard he is working for his business, but in some cases, priority has to be set and, in this case, this appointment should have been a priority. He did say that things were going well and there had been great inflow. I understand that he has to build his business but there are things you set out time for, and these antenatal appointments are one of them.

"I just got caught up. Won't happen again." He looks ahead as he drives, his finger gripping the steering so tightly that the muscles in his arms bulge.

I stare at them for a while, my heart pounding. I look from his arms to his face with his unkempt hair and a part of me feels torn.

I want to ask again what the problem is, I want to understand why he has been so distant. But I harden my face and force myself to stay quiet. I have asked too many a time that asking again would be insulting to me. If he does not wish to be open about what is going on, seeing that I am willing to listen, he should not let it affect me. This pregnancy alone has been challenging. My business has also been down because I do not have the energy to implement proper marketing strategies. I have just been quiet. My family has come around to accept my pregnancy but the rest of the world has not. So, the last thing I need is Tobore's issues encroaching on mine, especially because they are a mystery.

12

Tobore's attitude worsens and it upsets me. Our delivery due date is less than a month away so my belly has protruded hugely. And just when I thought nothing worse could happen, the strike gets called off.

I am sitting in the living room with Daddy, my leg on his lap as he massages it with olive oil (which he calls anointed oil) while we watch the news. Mummy is making jollof rice and the aroma of fried chicken wafts into the living room. I stare at the TV, astonished by the abruptness of the news. Daddy's hand on my feet pauses a bit before it continues. The TV sound fades out, and soon I am alone in a vast silence.

"What do you intend to do after giving birth?" Daddy asks and I hear him clearly as though we had walked together, handin-hand, into the vast silence. I feel his hand still rubbing my feet.

I decided to take things slowly after the overwhelming nature of the early stage of this pregnancy, so I hardly thought about postpregnancy. I am silent for a while, my mind racing.I hardly thought about post-pregnancy.

"You must return to Benin and finish your education," Daddy says finally. "You must get your degree. While we support in ways we can, you and Tobore must plan your lives to fit into each other's lives," he pauses, "while we hope on the future." He pauses again.

My breathing is heavy.

"But your education is important so that you can earn well. After that, we can speak of a proper marriage for you. You would marry, and be a good mother and wife."

Being female in this modern age means the stakes are higher for you. You have to excel at everything—education, career, motherhood, wifehood... everything. And so, you are saddled with this weight that everything must turn out well, that to fail to meet up to these expectations means you have failed at life.

"Yes sir," I say. He looks straight at the television and keeps watching. Mummy comes in a few minutes later with a tray that holds three plates of jollof rice. I lift my feet from Daddy's thighs onto the floor and sit up.

"Careful," Mummy warns.

When I am properly seated, I see that she is eyeing my stomach. "What do you intend to name your baby? Have you thought about that?"

I shake my head. "Not really."

"You should. Thinking and planning saves you a lot of confusion and stress about what to call the baby before you put to bed. Pray about it too, it'll come to you."

I do not pray about the name nor think about it because the days that follow become tedious. I do not want Tobore to follow me to the hospital for the next appointment so, I call Belema and ask her to accompany me.

"Ha, omo. If you had called me earlier, Petite, I would have been there for you. But I am on my way to Yaba as we speak."

I can hear the wind breezing against her voice and her phone microphone.

"Oh. Okay, don't worry; I'll go alone."

"Omo, you sound down. This Tobore thing... is really getting to you. Shey I will not rough him up like this?"

I laugh. "Nah, it's fine."

"Hmm... because since you said you've asked him many times and he is not saying anything, I really don't know. Men need to learn to be more open."

"I tire," I say, stepping out of the house and closing the door behind me.

"Abi you'll just go with Ned? He is heading to my house and is free for the rest of today." Her words come out so casually that I almost miss them. The name, Ned, sounds so distant because, for a long time, he did not exist in my consciousness. So, I smile at the realisation that I have moved past the *incident*. I imagine that going with Ned will be better than going alone.

"Are you sure?" I ask.

"Which kain yeye question be that?"

"Alright. Tell him for me, abeg," I plead, biting my lips.

"No wahala," Belema says.

Ned calls soon and then I order a ride and pick him up at Agungi Bus Stop. He smells of cool musk and is leaner than the last time I saw him. His eyes widen when he sees my belly.

"Wow, wow!" He laughs and claps.

I find his reaction amusing. "What?" I say with a chuckle.

"You look, really—big." He shakes his head, then averts my gaze. "And beautiful," he adds.

I hold my breath momentarily. I suddenly miss hearing Tobore call me beautiful while he stares into my eyes.

"Thank you," I nod. We drive past the Civic Centre and the driver makes a turn to the left. "You look good yourself. NYSC is almost over, so I guess, congratulations in advance."

He rubs his hand over his face. "Mehn, I cannot wait. I want all this to be over so I can move on. Plus, the company plans to retain me," he says and grins.

I hit his forearm lightly. "What? That is amazing news."

He shakes his head dramatically. "Guy! I felt the same way."

Securing stable employment in this country usually proves to be difficult, but here is Ned doing it. It is something to be happy about. When we arrive at the hospital, Ned insists on paying for the ride. He even rushes over to open the door for me. I am laughing as I alight because of his theatrics. He hooks our hands together and walks me into the hospital.

"We have to be careful. We cannot have a queen such as yourself bumping into anything. Ah han."

He rushes forward and pushes the door open for me and I walk through it grinning. Then he comes around to walk with me and winks as he does so.

"I did not know you were this funny," I said.

I am laughing so hard when we reach the counter, and it's *the* receptionist who stands behind the desk. Her gaze flits between Ned and I.

Dr Isioma is surprised to see Ned. She asks of Tobore. I tell her that he is busy. She asks that I send him her regards. She reminds me that my due date draws near and hopes that I am ready. She holds my hand and tells me that it is going to be a safe delivery. I do not doubt her. We are practising breathing exercises when Nelson enters the room and openly winks at Dr Isioma, who shakes her head.

"Pharm," she says.

"Sorry, sorry. I'll head out soon. Just wanted to remind you about tonight. My phone is acting up," Nelson says.

Dr Isioma looks at Ned and me briefly, reclines in her chair, and nods.

"I remember. I'll... be there," she says.

I turn towards Nelson and he is staring at me.

"You won't be there, right?"

He declares rather than asks. I do not know what he is talking about and he must have seen the confusion on my face.

"Eko Hotel dinner," he says. I shrug.

"No one told me," I say. They all must have assumed that I could not be there, not with my pregnancy. But it does not matter:

I already know who Dr Isioma is to Nelson.

When Nelson leaves, I look at Dr Isioma and shake my head.

"At least you're calm. You can be the cold water to his hot one."

She guffaws. It is the first time I have seen her laugh so loudly and openly. It is also the first time I acknowledge her relationship with my brother. We smile at each other but do not discuss the topic further. After the checkup, Ned suggests we grab ice cream from Cold Stone. I am reluctant about the idea at first, but when I recall that I would go home to stay alone and stare at my phone, waiting for Tobore to send a text, I accept. He pays for the ice cream, and we sit beside the entrance door because I want to be as close as possible to the air conditioner.

"Not everyone can look this good in pregnancy," he says, eyeing me, then raises a spoonful of chocolate ice cream to his lips. His eyes are a clear white and it is as though his thoughts are visible. I feel a shiver, so I look away and ignore his comment.

I scoop a spoonful of my mixed banana and vanilla-flavoured ice cream and shove it into my mouth.

"Omo, I miss secondary school sometimes, you know?" I say, to break what feels like an awkward silence.

"Ha, I do too sometimes! I think I enjoyed SS3 the most because being a prefect was really nice." He smirks and his eyes brighten.

"I was not a prefect sha. Didn't really know book like that, so," I shrug and titter.

"Come on. You used to try na. Didn't you win a prize for best in one subject one year like that?"

I raise both my brows. "Me?" I could never have won anything. I usually took one of the bottom ten positions at the end of school terms. It was not as if I did not work hard; I just never did well at examinations. Writing and providing explanations had never been my strengths. I improved academically, however, the year I wrote JUPEB.

Ned waves his hand. "Maybe it's just my imagination." Then he clears his throat. "But, really, you were so fine in secondary school. I used to see you walk past my classroom carrying that your small figure with confidence."

"With my flat yansh and flat chest that year." I laugh out loud, attracting stares, so I clamp my hand over my mouth. Ned continues laughing and makes no effort to retrain himself. "I still had a crush on you with all that flatness." "Abegi," I scoff.

"I'm serious, Zee. I did. It was why I even wanted to talk to you at that event. I was like, Damn! she grew even more beautiful." He gazes at me, his eyes still cloudy. He licks the ice cream slowly and I watch his hand lift a spoonful to his mouth, his mouth opening, and his tongue lapping at the ice cream. He blinks and I catch myself.

I know this conversation should not go further, so I shake my head.

"We really should start going. Omo, I do not want to get stuck in VGC traffic with the Uber price going up." "Yeah, true," he says.

We stand up at the same time. Just as we approach the exit of Cold Stone, I feel an acute pain on the left side of my belly. I pause, staring down at my stomach. I stop abruptly. I feel a sharper pain, as though I am being stabbed with a long pin.

Ned is close enough so that he reaches and touches the small of my back.

"Are you all right?"

I shake my head, tittering because, somehow, I know what is happening.

"I think the baby is kicking."

Ned stands straighter; his hand relaxes on my back. Then he laughs.

"That is so great. This is the first kick, yeah?"

"Yes." I look up at him and nod. Then, I remember Tobore asking about this the last time he followed me to the hospital. Maybe he had wanted to be there when this kick happened. If he wants to be here, then he should have remembered the appointment. He should be here. Not Ned, not anyone else, Tobore!

"Hey, why do you look pissed?" Ned asks. I shrug.

The kicking has stopped, but the sting lingers. I stand straight.

"Order a ride, please. Let's go."

"You look agitated," Ned says. He does not bring out his phone to order a ride. "You can talk to me, Zee."

I stare at him. What does he want me to talk about? Do I confess that, even this late in the pregnancy, I am not ready to be a mother? Or that I am scared that I may die during childbirth? Or that I am disappointed in myself for being pregnant without being married? I don't even have a name for the child yet. I do not see a picture of myself carrying this child or breastfeeding it. My life after having this baby is a seemingly impenetrable fog. Do I tell him that the future petrifies me?

I am unable to form the words. Instead, tears gather at the corner of my eyes and I find myself leaning into Ned, and he embraces me and I let myself cry.

"I'm not ready for this baby, Ned. I am so scared. What if I die? Or the baby dies?"

"Shh," he rubs my head. Then rests his head on my forehead. "No bad thoughts, Zee. No bad thoughts. Nothing will happen to your baby. Nothing. You need to start seeing the positive side of everything. You chose to keep this baby—" "An influenced choice," I cut in.

Ned moves away slightly, his hand around my shoulder but his gaze on me.

"Irrespective of how that choice was made, Zee, you made it. You have kept the baby. So, you must work towards ensuring that this baby is not going to pay for anything. Make sure that the baby has love and family. Whatever circumstances that led here are not the baby's fault. You must always remember this."

It used to be Tobore doing this, but with Ned standing here today, doing and saying all these, it just makes me miss Tobore even more. But how do I speak to someone who does not want to be spoken to.

13

Ned continues to check up on me in the days after the checkup. He texts me frequently, and even when I do not respond, he does not falter. But his texts are not the ones I yearn for, so, most times, I do not respond. Until one night, when Sobenne's soft snores keep me awake, I decide to go through my unread WhatsApp messages and Ned's text comes in.

Ned: *What's up?*

I stare at the message for a while, wondering if I should respond. I sigh.

Me: *I dey.*

His response comes quickly before I can leave the chat and pretend to be busy elsewhere, so delay my response.

Ned: *How come you are still awake at this time?*

Me: *Couldn't sleep. You?*

Ned: *Trying to look through my Snapchat* Me: *Oh, nice. Have fun.*

I leave the chat and open some group messages. I consider texting Belema but she is not online and she has not responded to the last message I sent to her. She is so busy with work these days that she barely has time for anything else. I cannot wait to be done with the pregnancy so I can focus on my business again.

Ned's message pops up.

Ned: *I just saw something on snap that I think you might relate to.*

Beneath the message is a video of a pregnant lady in a red top-bra and a mum's jeans, drawing on her round belly. The end product of the drawing looks like an image of Humpty Dumpty. I muffle a guffaw with my palm.

Me: *Na wa o, this is so hilarious. Maybe I would try it, see what it looks like. But I can't even use a black marker. My stomach is so dark ehn.*

Ned: *Send to me when you do abeg, I wan laugh. That is normal for you.*

It will clear up after the baby. Still not sleepy?

Me: *Nah, and I don't know why.*

My phone vibrates almost immediately. Ned is calling. I swipe to answer. "Why are you calling me so late?"

"You said you couldn't sleep. Thought you might need company."

"E-hen; Sorry o, Good Samaritan," I tease.

He laughs. Then he clears his throat.

"So, B refused to tell me, but I am curious. Did you and Tobore have a fight?"

His question shocks me and I feel ambushed by the abruptness of it. But it is late at night, and Tobore is a question that troubles me, so I decide to talk about it.

"I... uhm... he just started acting strange." I go on to tell Ned how it all started and how till now, Tobore is still distant and the only thing we talk about is the baby. Everything else we used to talk about, how close we used to be, it all changed.

"He is just so far away it feels like I can't reach him."

Ned clears his throat. "Honestly, ehn, I was surprised when I heard you were pregnant for him. I have not really seen any chemistry between you two. And up until now, you guys are not even in a relationship."

"Ned, that is not the point. And the fact that we are not in a relationship does not mean that we don't like each other," I say matter-of-factly.

"I know, Zee. I just feel like maybe everything is happening too fast and maybe the only reason you both might have been trying to make things work is because of the baby."

I sigh. He is right. I kissed Tobore that day at the park because I wanted to speed things up. I just wanted him at our house because I wanted my parents to see that Tobore and I could eventually be something, and that could mend my relationship with them. But after that, I started to actually like Tobore even more. And this is why his distance hurts so much.

"No, Ned. I really do like Tobore, baby aside. And I would never sleep with someone I do not feel any sort of emotional connection to. There just has to be something there in the first place."

"I feel you. Well, maybe things are overwhelming on his end. You just need to give it time."

Everyone says the same thing, but it is difficult to be on the receiving end of Tobore's recent behaviour.

"Can we just talk about something else?" I ask, sighing.

"Sure," Ned says excitedly. He begins to tell me NYSC stories. I laugh at all the camp stories, knowing I will also experience them sometime soon. Ned talks about Mami market, waking up before sunrise. He tells me about NYSC romances. He keeps talking until I fall asleep. The next day, while everyone has gone to work and I am home listening to a podcast for new mothers on YouTube, one of the links Tobore had shared, I feel an inclination to draw on my stomach.

I stand naked before the long mirror in the corridor. Everything about me has changed. My thighs are thicker, my hips, wider and darker. My belly is so big and dark, with a black line drawn down its centre. I look like a stranger to myself. My stomach astounds me so much that I chuckle. It is incredulous how much a woman's body can stretch.

I think about my vagina eventually stretching and I shudder. My phone rings. It is Ned. I smile. With everyone busy, it feels like he is there for me to talk to and that offers a lot of comfort.

"What's up?"

"Wanted to ask how you're doing. I saw a pregnant woman and thought of you."

I laugh, holding my breasts as I do because my rumbling makes them ache.

In the following days, while my mates prepare to resume school and my due date draws near, Ned becomes my primary confidant. He calls and texts frequently, and also keeps me updated about how things are going with him. Sometimes, he has goodies delivered to me at home. He asks for bump pictures on Snap and, because of him, I begin to use my Snapchat app more frequently.

Tobore and I talk less and less. Sometimes he would recall that we have visits and call to check up on me. The calls increasingly get awkward. He still sends me reels on pregnancy and motherhood, most of which I watch, because they keep me informed and so, a little less uncertain about what to expect.

Daddy buys new baby items almost every day and keeps them in the room we have prepared as a nursery. He seems so excited about the baby's impending arrival and I am thrilled to watch him being so excited. It warms my heart when he comes home and sings out for me.

"Zimi, zimi, Nwa mma oh!" He calls out.

I am sitting on the floor of my room, one of the books Tobore bought for me about motherhood open on my lap. Daddy's voice makes me giggle, and I stand and head downstairs. Daddy stands at the bottom of the stairs, holding up a bunch of yellow bananas.

"Your favourite fruit in your favourite colour."

In his other hand is a large black nylon bag. "Your mummy and I went shopping."

I climb down the stairs carefully, smiling. As I get closer to him, my cheeks begin to hurt. I hear cluttering in the kitchen and I know it is Mummy. I reach Daddy and embrace him. He plants a kiss on my forehead and rests his head against mine. Mummy comes out from the kitchen, sucking on oranges.

"Thank you, Mummy. Thank you, Daddy." I am giggling.

Mummy comes forward and touches my shoulder before climbing up the staircase.

"At least we did not need to buy much since our son-in-law has sent a majority of what we need."

I swallow as I pull away from Daddy. Son-in-law? Perhaps Daddy sees the look on my face, or the question is on his mind.

"And how is Tobore? I have not been seeing him around recently. Hope all is well?" He asks

"Yes, yes," I say. I swallow hard.

"Two of you are fine?" Daddy asks, his brows raised. His lips are parted slightly but I am certain that my answer will determine whether or not they curl into a smile or compress for a frown. And what happens if I just clarify that Tobore and I are not together? At this point, I am tired of all that has been demanded of me throughout this pregnancy. But I do not know what reaction Daddy would have to my confession that Tobore and I are no longer together—we never were, in the first place— but Daddy would be disappointed. After all, the only reason he and Mummy came around was because Tobore started showing up at the house and acting all lovey.

"Yes, daddy. We are fine."

His lips curl into a smile. He pats my back and then climbs up the stairs. I stand there, staring ahead. I decide to go for a walk. I call Belema on my way out.

"Petite baby," she says, dragging each syllable, and I know instantly that she is high. I nearly groan.

"Belema, what's up? Are you good?"

"Yeah..." she says slowly and pauses. When she is high, her character becomes a contrast to her original personality. I like to look at her when she is high, so I can laugh at how tranquil she looks.

"I'm fine... I'm trying to work... It's flowing..." She chuckles.

I also know that she gets high when she is not inspired to work and she needs a push. She has had a busy schedule.

"That is good, good."

"Yeah... Are you fine? Do you want to talk?"

I consider whether to let her work or share my problems with her. I want to let her work, but I also know that I may not find her this calm and focused again for days. Or she might be too busy to pick up my calls.

"This Tobore issue, it's stressing me. How can someone just switch up like that?"

Belema is quiet for a while. Then she speaks.

"Ah-han... He's still acting that way?"

"Yes na," I groan. "The same. And now, my dad is already asking questions about him. What am I supposed to say?"

I walk past a house that used to be painted white but now is blue. I wonder when it was repainted.

Belema scoffs.

"Is that really what you are worried about now, Zimi? I think that is the last thing that should worry you. Really."

"Well, yes. Because the more everyone begins to notice his absence then—"

"So Zimi, na only this thing dey bother you since this matter start? Have you always only been bothered by how his behaviour is affecting you?"

"What? No. You have been here since this issue started. I told you that I asked many times and he would not answer."

"I sabi. But... What I'm asking is if you really worry for him."

I frown and nod. "Yes."

Belema chuckles. "No, Petite. You don't. Fuck... See me dey blame the man since o. Say na him no wan open up."

Irked by the way she is recasting this whole issue, I rub my temples and groan. "What the fuck are you even saying?"

"When you started this thing, I ask you say shey you really like this guy and you tell me yes, Zim. And I left you. Don't you think that everything is backfiring now?" "How?" I ask, irritated.

"Maybe what is going on with him does not even involve you at all at all, that he doesn't know how to tell you because he doesn't feel that you truly care. Maybe he feels used. On the other hand, maybe you don't know how to ask him in a way that shows you care, because what you care about is not Tobore but your situation with him and how it looks." She speaks so slowly and smoothly I am irritated even more.

"You're just talking high talk, Belema," I say, shaking my head. I recall telling her before that I have asked Tobore *severally* what the problem is and he has refused to respond. Would I have asked that many times if I did not care?

"No... No."

"Belema, just go back to work, you hear? I will text you later."

She hums a response, and I hang up. I stand under the masquerade tree in the estate park, staring into the distance. I see the colourful playground for children. I watch a boy and a girl running around in the playground. I find myself stroking my belly.

14

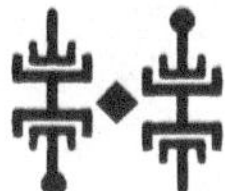

The void created by Tobore's absence is so wide even Ned's friendship cannot fill it. I feel pain in my chest each time I see a reel from Tobore on my phone or when his bland text comes in. I keep wondering to myself what went wrong. If I were not pregnant, and his bland messages and reels were not coming in, I would have been able to say I was being ghosted. Although I wish I could ask him what happened to us, but I fear the answer I may get.

"Eat more fruits. I have not seen you eat any in the past week."

Mummy places a bowl of pineapple and watermelon cut into small chunks before me on the dining table. It is one of those weeks when her usual workload lightens, so she decides to check on her pregnant daughter.

Sobenne has gone out and Daddy is attending a meeting with his townspeople somewhere on the mainland.

Mummy pulls a chair out from opposite me and sits down. She has a bowl of fruits before her as well.

"Tobore stopped coming around."

I freeze momentarily. "Yes—" I begin to say but get stuck.

"You should do whatever it takes to have him by your side, Nne. So that when he is financially stable, he will remember that he has to marry you. Otherwise, finding a husband would not be easy." She spits watermelon seeds into her hand and drops them onto the empty plate beside her bowl of fruits.

"Around that time we discovered your pregnancy, your sister was talking to one man. He was very serious about her, so serious." My interest piques, so I chew slower.

"The man really liked her and wanted to marry her. Sobenne liked him o, very much in fact." I wonder how Mummy knows all this. I doubt that Sobenne actually opened up to her. Maybe Sobenne told Nelson, and then Nelson told Mummy.

"Sobe found out the man has a son with another woman, so she turned him down. Now, I don't even understand the story properly, but it seems Sobe feels that the man is still attached to this other woman. But I'm sure it's either the lady is pushing him away or she has not proven to be a good wife material for the man. It's good for a lady to keep her head down so that the man can see the good in you. Men don't have a problem. They are easy to figure out. All you need do is be good to them. The only reasons you should let a man slip from your hands are if he hits you or if he cheats, which most of them do anyway. But for these two things, carry your slippers and run. Even the Bible says it. Because Umu nwoke ehn—" she pauses to chew some watermelon.

"Aside from that, I see no other problem. You are a beautiful girl, well-behaved; you cook well, you clean up well, and you are hardworking. Sharp business acumen." She taps my hand, her eyes wide. "If you want to keep Tobore, you will. He is soft. He's a good man. All he needs is someone he's sure will be good to him."

"Sobenne is looking for a husband now, Nne. It bothers her and it bothers me too. Well educated, finished strong, and has a good job, omara mma nwanyi, my Sobe is stunning, gorgeous. She is an intelligent girl, but now she needs a husband. What do her qualities matter later in life if she has no family of her own? Your own path is different, following a direction that our people will frown upon. But, surely, all will be well. For that to happen, you must work."

I stare at mummy. I wonder when Sobenne was going through all these and I did not know. She never told me anything. I frown. No one tells me anything anymore. When was Sobenne going through heartbreak that I did not notice? But then, Sobenne tends to keep things about her to herself.

When she returns home, I am in the room and it is late at night. I sit up. She kicks her pumps off and removes her honeyblonde wig. The room smells of her perfume, and her light skin looks a bit darker, tanned by the Lagos sun.

"Ah-han, you're still awake?" She says. She takes off her wristwatch and tosses it onto the bed.

"Yeah," I say. "Can we talk?"

She frowns and comes to sit beside me on the bed. "What's the matter, Baby? Are you alright?"

"Mummy and I talked today." I swallow. She squints her eyes at me. "She mentioned that you had a breakup. A-are you fine? I'm really sorry I did not know you were going through that."

Sobenne's shoulders relax, and her face rearranges into sadness so apparent that her lips appear to be straight. "Yes, I am going through a heartbreak, Zimi." She looks away.

"But I'll be fine. It's not the end of the world. I mean, I loved him, but I know it's better to walk away from what I have seen than to get married and allow myself to get hurt when his emotions lead him to act."

"I suppose Nelson was the one who gave the gist to Mummy?"

Sobe shakes her head. "I did. When she was bugging me about marriage. And then she noticed my mood wasn't great."

"Typical Mummy." I chuckle. "But when was your mood that down? You that you know how to hide how you feel. You are either always in the kitchen or—"

Sobenne scoffs. "Hide how I feel? E-hen... For the past few weeks, I have been so down. Even in the kitchen. I could not possibly hide it because I was so pained." She shakes her head. "Well, it's probably only you who did not notice. But you never notice anything anyway."

I am taken aback. "What?"

She shrugs. "You never notice anything. Your mind is just not there-there. Or maybe you notice and you never speak about things, I don't know."

I want to ask more, but then Sobe yawns and groans and I remember she must be exhausted, so I let the matter go. I have something else I want to discuss with Sobenne.

"Mummy is bugging me too about Tobore. I don't even know what to do about that. But somehow, I wonder if she is right about me, you know, trying to keep him. If he slips away—"

"Calm down o," Sobenne cuts in and stares at me. "What are you saying? Keep him? As per, he's a toy?"

"No. Just... having him around. I like him."

"That I'm sure of. But, apparently, you're more concerned about what everyone is saying than about your feelings, his feelings, and your compatibility."

I am shocked again and feel hurt. That is an extreme conclusion. "What?"

"Yes, Baby. Tobore distanced himself but you were more focused on the fact of losing his attention than on why he withdrew. And maybe that is part of the reason he has remained withdrawn from you."

I stare at her, my mouth agape. Sobenne stares at me pointedly, as though daring me to counter her, to defend myself.

"You have ghosted him many times. And he still made efforts to keep in touch. I've not seen you really showing you care about him, Zimife. You have to figure out what you want at this stage of your life. Remember we talked about this before: set your priorities right. Know what comes first. Don't do anything because anyone is pressuring you. It will backfire. Figure yourself out."

She stands and begins to undress. I stare at the *Glam Girl* logo on the wall, my heart heavy.

A lot of my preoccupations in the past months have been about myself and how I can make people stop judging me: the receptionist at the hospital, Mummy and Daddy, the women at church; how I could avoid questions that may arise about me getting pregnant before marriage. I hardly let myself think about this baby, about his or her place in my life, about being a mother.

How am I supposed to be a mother if I do not plan for it? Ned's words come to mind.

Irrespective of how that choice was made, Zee, you made it. You have kept the baby. So, you must work towards ensuring that this baby is not going to pay for anything. Make sure that the baby has love and family. Whatever circumstances that led here is not the baby's fault. You must always remember this.

I think of Tobore making all those plans, sending those books, making such efforts. All I have been is ungrateful.

The next day, I am on a call with Belema, and I tell her what Sobenne says.

"Well, there are two ways to look at this, Petite. You said you tried to talk to him, but he pushed you away. And when you called, he came immediately."

"Yeah?" I say, peeling the banana mummy gave me before everyone left for church.

"He was patient with you and, I don't know, I feel like you tried, really. You ask am more than twice now, so wetin dey do am?"

"Exactly," I say quickly, dropping the banana on the plate. "I asked him o."

"But still, maybe you never asked in a way that made him feel like you cared. Maybe you asked because it was affecting you, not because you wanted to know."

I slouch on the chair and groan. "How is that any different?"

"It is, Petite. Think about it. If it did not affect you, or affect his affection towards you, would you have asked?"

I stand up from the dining table and walk into the living room. The alarm blares just as light illuminates the room. My eyes wander until it settles on the Virgin Mary figurine. I look away from her and shake my head.

"I guess I would have just waited until he came around." I think of Sobenne. I knew she was going through something, but I forgot to ask. And I simply ignored it sometimes. If it affected me, I would have asked before Mummy told me.

"Fuck, I should have tried harder, been more encouraging. Do you know how many times he sends me Instagram and YouTube links to help me feel better? Even the books he sent to me. Guy, I feel terrible." I stomp my feet.

"Normally," Belema affirms, "You suppose feel bad. You mess up. And you just dey tell me story from your side. Come be like say na our guy dey guilty."

"Belema," I warn.

"It's the truth, Petite."

I rub my temple. "Enough about me. How are you?"

"I dey o. I have been busy here and there sha. But Ned don dey behave somehow."

"How?"

"I no know. He just acts somehow these days. Distant. Maybe it's because I have been busy."

I think Ned is an excellent communicator. He has been a good talker on our calls and texts. And even at the beginning of their relationship, Belema commended this. So, what might be the problem now?

Ned and I talk better than we used to, so, it would be good for me to dig around about his situation with Belema, because I want to make sure that he does absolutely nothing to hurt her.

"I'm sure it's because you are both preoccupied, Babe. Talk to him about it. You always talk about things."

"Yeah." She sighs. "I will. I'm also sorry I haven't visited or called in a while. I've been really busy. I'm making bridesmaid dresses for a wedding at the end of November. So, I really need to be done early so I can go for the fitting and know it's final. And at least, have pocket money to resume school with." "And also save o," I remind her.

"Yes, Petite. Of course."

"Pele," I mutter. "Your hard work will pay off."

"Ah, it has to o. You know it is me and you that will spend the money."

"I know na!" And we both laugh.

"When are you going back to school?" I ask.

She lets out a short laugh.

"They've released calendar mehn… Did you see how cramped it is?"

"I saw it o. I just laughed. Class group chat don blow up," I guffaw.

"Why e no go blow up? Course rep don dey message lecturers. That reminds me: remember we need to see Dr Lawanson about your result."

I stare down at my stomach and scoff. "Have to give birth first before I see him."

"Well, yeah. But you'd be due in two weeks. After you born, life goes on. And we go surely navigate everything," Belema assures me. Her voice is like a resounding bell, reminding me that there is nothing I cannot do.

"Yes, yes. Sure."

"Omo, I have to get ready for the memorial tomorrow."

I sigh. Tomorrow is the 20th of October, two years since the massacre of #EndSars protesters at the Lekki Toll Gate. I stare at my belly.

"Go for two, B." I sigh.

"Of course, baby. It's for two… Three actually," she says and giggles

I guffaw. "Three, yes."

"So, about your question, I can only resume after your delivery. I have to be here for that shit, watch you push a baby from your puna—"

"Belema!" I cut in and we both laugh, my body rumbling as we do. The baby kicks and my laughter gets louder. I stroke my belly, my heart beating rapidly at the thought of actually pushing out the baby. I hope Belema is right, that after the child is born, life can go on.

After the call, I send a message to Ned concerning Belema. I feel that we are in a more comfortable space for me to ask him on my friend's behalf. After all, he had asked about Tobore.

Me: *Hey, what's up?*

His response comes quickly.

Ned: *I dey, you? Good??*

Me: *Yeah, I am fine. I just spoke to Belema. What is it I hear about you both not communicating?*

Ned: *Lol, Z. Is it really comfortable to talk to you about my relationship?*

Me: *Says the person who asked about mine.*

Three dots indicate that he is typing, but soon the dots vanish. I wait a bit and they pop back up. His response comes in.

Ned: *Well, you have a point. But really, I don't know tbh. I just feel like we rarely talk and I don't know how to fix it.*

Me: *Tell her that. My friend is very responsive. And she has been crazy busy, so make the extra effort abeg.*

Ned: *I will talk to her about it when you talk to Tobore.*

I roll my eyes at his message.

Me: *How did that even come up?*

Ned: *No deal then.*

Me: *What are you even saying??*

Ned: *I feel that you and that guy need to talk about what is going on, and set the right boundaries and all. No matter what, you both are raising a baby.*

I want to respond to him about his idea that I need to set boundaries with Tobore. Ned seems to believe that Tobore and I might be forcing things or that I am doing all of this from desperation. I feel like I need to clear the air, but then, I do not want to drag the conversation with him.

I begin to think about Tobore. I may not have been sure of my feelings for him at first, but his absence in the past weeks has made it clear to me. My heart skips when I read his message, when I hear his voice somewhere, and even when I watch the silly videos I have of him. Our picture from the photoshoot is the first thing I see when I pick my phone up: he staring down at me while my smile is sunny. Sometimes I hear his voice in my head. *Sissy, come on. I got you banana bread. Are you good? Make it a great day.* Sometimes it is as if I can smell his perfume or feel his hand caressing me. I miss Tobore and I wonder if he misses me too. I stare at the phone now.

Unwilling to argue, but very much willing to strike this deal.

Me: *Deal. I talk to Tobore and you talk to Belema.*

He responds with a dancing sticker. *Great!*

15

I visit Tobore on his birthday. I had texted earlier to wish him a happy birthday and to ask if he was at home. He replied that he was and that he wanted me to come over. I would have arrived there earlier, but I sneezed on my way out, causing pee to wet my underwear. I groaned all the way back up and down the stairs.

It is late afternoon when I arrive at Tobore's. His house looks and feels different, darker. Tobore sits in the living room, a glass of wine in his hand. His hair is freshly cut, his beard relined, but his eyes are exhausted. I presume he had decided to look good for his birthday despite whatever has weighed him down.

He looks *edible*, despite the fatigue and melancholy he wears. From the door, I can smell his perfume—a mix of cool musk and vanilla. At first, I could not stop staring at him. I want to kiss him, run my tongue up and down his face, holding him close to me, resting his head on my chest, his hand on my waist. And those plump lips devouring mine.

I bring with me his favourite chocolates, Maltesers, a bottle of wine and some doughnuts. I place them on the dining table while he is rushing over to meet me. He hugs me with one hand while the other holds up the glass cup. His hug is lifeless and that hurts me.

I move back, my hands in my back pockets. I stare at his feet in yellow crocs and raise my head sharply to meet his gaze. He smiles.

"They reminded me of you, so I got them."

I cannot hold back my laughter. "Bro!"

He shakes his head. "Uh-uh... don't do that," he says, shaking his head.

I raise my hands in the air. "Sorry, sorry. Incest, I know." I smile at him and we are quiet briefly.

"Happy Birthday, Tobore." I nod towards the things on the dining table. His eyes trail after mine.

His smile is so wide when he looks back at me. I can feel his happiness, and that thrills me. He bites his lower lip for a second.

"Thank you, Sissy."

Then, as though he had just snapped back to his senses, he shakes his head and gestures to the couch.

"Shit, sorry; come sit, Sissy."

I can tell that the air is lighter now, his tone calm and even. But I know what happens when we begin like this: we fall into a normal routine and everything goes on as if the past few weeks did not happen. We start feeling each other again and we just feel our way back to where we were before the last few weeks happened, until one person ghosts again or something pushes us apart.

"What happened, Tobore?" I am still standing when I ask him this.

He turns to face me. His brows shoot up. He downs the rest of the wine, drops the glass and rubs his hand behind his black shorts. He presses his lips together, just as his eyes meet mine.

"I don't want to—"

"No, we have to. Because you like me and I like you. Because we are having a baby together. And, most importantly, because I care about you," I blurt. My chest heaves as I stand there looking at him, searching his demeanour.

Tobore nods, claps his hands together and holds them there.

"I don't even know if I'm ready to let you in on this, because I'm still dealing with it. And I don't want you to have to think of me like this."

I want to say something, but I pause, trying to tread carefully. Then I laugh. He raises an eyebrow at me. I shake my head.

"Sorry, I wanted to say that relationships are all about communication. But I guess I cannot even say that because we don't know yet what we are. And maybe that's part of the problem. Because you shift away from me when you are going through something. Whereas, in a true relationship, you should be able to share both good and bad times."

Tobore nods, a ghost of a smile appearing on his lip.

"Yeah, Sissy. You're right. But I'm also not sure we're in the position for a proper relationship."

I am hurt that he thinks that, and I am certain that I bear this hurt on my face, because he sighs and swallows. I shake my head, trying to remind myself that this is not about me. What he is going through is much bigger than me and I need to see things from his point of view instead of arguing right now.

"Look, before the pregnancy, you did not want a relationship with me but I hung around because I was hopeful. But, after the pregnancy, I was unable to see a line between you wanting a relationship because I am your baby daddy, or because you genuinely developed feelings for me."

My lips part but no words come out.

"Don't get me wrong, my being distant recently is not about that. But since we are speaking about it, then I think I owe you this honesty. I really really like you, Zim. But I want your liking me to be genuine and not based on our baby but it kind of felt like it was many times—"

"It isn't," I cut in. I shake my head, feeling overwhelmed. My palms are sweaty and my dress suddenly feels too tight.

Tobore smiles.

"I like you, baby. I do. But can we not define this until we move past a certain stage?"

"What stage? I want to know what we're doing now. I don't want to be in that situation where I don't know how to talk to you. As a girlfriend or as a baby mama? What are my boundaries as your baby mama?" I hit my forehead with my palm. "I cannot believe I now refer to myself as such."

"After the baby," he says. He stuffs his hands in the pocket of the shorts.

It is a reasonable timeline. The baby is coming soon and that would give us just enough time.

"Good, but we surely are still the way we were, yeah?" My eyes are pleading. He is the only form of intimacy that I have and I like him, which makes intimacy with him the only one I seek.

"Yeah," he smirks. "The way we were."

I am so giddy I want to run to him. I remember that I need to know what had happened to him. I clear my throat and look away from him.

"Irrespective of what we choose to define this as you are also my friend and because of this child, we would have to be friends for life. So, you should be open when you are going through stuff. You matter to me. And I came here to know what actually happened to you. Because I want to know. Because I care about you."

His gaze softens as it meets mine. His lips begin to move and I struggle to focus on his words at first.

"Sponsors started to pull out. The website was ready and we did a virtual launch. But money to push further became a problem. Everything I envisioned for the next five years began to unravel and was getting further away from me. My mind went crazy and then the dream Fintech company became only an imagination— something I could never do or achieve. I grew tired."

My legs begin to feel weak. I am astounded by his revelation, by this truth that I could have guessed so easily. The signs were apparent. I just ignored his pain and focused on being deprived of his attention. But why did he not even share this with me?

"I lost it, Zimi. I just felt useless. So, I wanted to be on my own."

"That was why you pushed me away?" I want to lash out about him not trusting me enough to tell me, that he could have just explained this to me rather than putting me through all that heartache. Then I remember what Mummy, Sobenne, and Belema said. Then I remember that this is not about me. It is about him. About what weighed on him so much for weeks, which he could not share. And I do not know the right words, but surely, they should not begin with me seeking explanations. They also cannot begin with "sorry" because I know he hates hearing that word when he is down. But I say it anyway.

"I'm sorry that happened to your company." I nod slowly.

"I think I needed that. To just hear someone tell me that." He smiles.

"Yeah?" I ask, confused.

"Yeah." He nods. "And maybe some boobs to rest my head on."

I shake my head and laugh. "This guy."

I walk over to him and stretch out my arms. He bends slightly to rest his head on my shoulder. His arms go around my waist and I feel that heat within me.

"Plan B. What's your plan B? You always have a plan B." "Plan B sucks," he mutters.

"Tell me."

"Get a job and work with my degree. And then there is plan C." He leans away from me and stares down at me. His tired eyes look brighter, not as gloomy as it was when I walked in.

"What's plan C? Go back to Plan A?"

He grins. "Exactly." He guides me to take a seat, then he sits beside me. "But I have to find a steady job—not just freelancing—while I work on the company."

"I agree."

He rests his head on my chest while I am leaning into the couch.

"I missed you," he murmurs.

"Why did you push me away?"

"I was fresh in the phase. I did not want you to be bothered about me. I was too angry at myself. Too consumed."

I understand this because I can be like that as well, pushing people away when I am in the depth of my pain. My legs feel cramped from sitting. I want to walk around. I tell Tobore and he sits up. I place my phone and purse beside him and walk to the dining table.

"Come, let us share your chocolate," I say

My phone beeps. The notification sound is from WhatsApp.

I am already unboxing the glazed doughnuts.

"Help me check, abeg. Might be from my school group chat," I say.

"Okay," Tobore says. I see him swiping my phone. The chocolate on the doughnut smears my hand.

He frowns as he swipes. My stained hands are held up.

"What is it?"

Tobore stares intently at whatever he is reading. His expression has changed so swiftly as though a switch has been flipped. His eyes seem ablaze when he looks up and stares at me. I gasp and take tentative steps towards him.

"What is it, Tobore?"

He hands me the phone and turns away.

"I'll call you an Uber." He is searching for his phone.

I hold my phone with the side of both hands, careful not to stain it with doughnut glaze. My Snapchat stares at me, the chats and saved snaps between Ned and me splayed open.

Ned: *Zim, how far?*

Above this message is a picture of me in shorts and a sports bra. My belly shines and my expression is weird and intended to be humorous. The image had been an effort to make Ned laugh. And Ned's response, reading it now, makes the entire message look like what it is not.

Ned: *Sexyyyyy mama. Even in pregnancy.*

Me: (A stupid blush emoji followed by) *Thank you Ned. Ikrr.*

I wonder how Tobore ended up on Snapchat in the first place. I swipe to my WhatsApp and then my shoulders slouch. Ned had messaged me on WhatsApp, just under our message about the deal.

Ned: *It has been days now o. What is your update on your own side of the bargain?*

I look up. Tobore is aggressively pressing his phone.

"Tobore," I call out meekly, my vice shaky.

"Your ride will be here soon."

"This is not what it looks like." I approach him. He catches my approach in the corner of his eyes and glares at me.

"Stay away from me!" He yells. His voice is so uncharacteristically loud and violent it startles me onto the spot.

My chest heaves and I feel dizzy with guilt.

"This means nothing!" I scream. "Ned and I are just friends."

Tobore stuffs one hand in his pocket while the other is pressing his phone.

"The ride will be here in eleven minutes. I don't have time for this."

"Tobore!" I scream.

"Zimife! You send him belly pictures. Belly pictures wey me wey be pikin papa never even see! And then you both make a deal? It was his deal that brought you here, not because you care. And all that bullshit you were saying about caring about me... And you dare to tell me it's not what it looks like?"

"Ned is just my friend. He was there for me when you were not," I glare at him. "Besides, he's Belema's boyfriend. I see nothing wrong in being friends with him."

"Look at you being in deliberate denial. Always nonchalant to the things happening around you. You were nonchalant about my feelings when I asked you then to be my girlfriend. Nonchalant about my hurt—"

"I see no reason why you are going back to the past. This isn't so deep," I say, irritated.

"I wish once in a while you could listen to yourself." He shakes his head. "See, ehn, I do not even have the energy to argue. My head is full and this is the last thing I want to add to it."

I shake my head, because I am convinced he is blowing it all out of context. He needs to calm down and see from my point of view that Ned is just my friend.

"Ned is just my friend. What is wrong with that?"

"Boundaries, Zimife. Boundries." Tobore scoffs. "This friendship you have with him has no boundary. No respect for Belema and me. Look at you using our relationship to make a deal with him. Does Belema know you both are this close? Does she know you two are so close you're sharing belly pictures with him?"

I feel the bottom of my stomach churn, and my head spins. I look back down at the phone and stare at the messages. I stare at Snapchat and the tone of the message. Ned and I indeed got too close. I look back up at Tobore.

"That's what I thought." Tobore nods.

My lower back stiffens with pain, and my abdomen tightens. This tightening is novel. It feels more painful, and the pain lasts longer. I grab my lower abdomen and squeeze my clothes there. "What is it? Are you fine?"

The pain comes sharply again, and this time I let out a painful grunt. "Jesus."

Tobore rushes to my side but he does not touch me. "Fuck, are you in labour?"

I shake my head, my eyes watering.

"I don't know... it's just so fucking painful." I groan.

Tobore begins to dial a number. He leads me to sit. As we walk to the couch, the pain lessens gradually. And then, it stops.

"Hello, Dr Isioma. Yes, she.. she is having contractions and she was not doing anything stressful." He walks around me while I stand before the couch, waiting for the pain to come again.

Tobore puts the call on speakerphone. "Zim, are the contractions regular?"

"It just stopped, and it has not come again. Will it come?"

"It might. But I want to make sure it is not labour contractions," Dr Isioma says. Her voice is muffled for a bit, but it becomes clearer.

"Did your water break? Or did you see any clear, pink or slightly bloody discharge?"

I look at Tobore, my heart thudding.

"Let me check, but I'm not feeling anything."

I turn to make my way to the restroom, but Tobore shakes his head.

"Check here," he mouths.

I swallow and slip my hand beneath the beige dress. I feel for any discharge and when I feel none, I tell her.

"Well, it's just Braxton Hicks again. And it's normal. You might feel it a lot more as the due date approaches," she says. "But you need to walk around a bit or change your position if you are doing anything stressful. You also need to not be under any kind of stress, please. I say this always but I am repeating it, okay?" "Okay." I nod, looking down at my swollen feet.

"Alright, take care." She hangs up.

Tobore releases a breath. "Thank God."

We stand in silence now, staring at each other. His eyes are dull again, and he is shaking his head.

"I think a good way for you to walk around is to just walk outside now and pace until the driver arrives."

He goes to wear the leather slippers placed by the door leading to his bedroom. I know that the moment I walk out of here, things will change again, and this time, maybe it will be worse, but I feel the need to try to clear the air, a need to be bold, and maybe, for the first time, to genuinely acknowledge what I know that I want.

"I'm sorry you saw what you saw the way you did. And maybe you are right that I sometimes seem nonchalant, but I genuinely took Ned only as a friend. And you are right. It got too far, maybe. I just sent the picture because he asked. I did not see anything wrong with it. I was not naked—"

"That is not the point," he says, his face hurt and tired. I feel stupid.

"I did not take it as anything serious. He was just there for me during the past few weeks when I couldn't get through to you. It meant nothing."

"You did not set boundaries with this dude. No respect for Belema or me. Because you fucking knew that we had something. Jesus, Zimife! Are you listening to what you're saying? You have not even accepted that your friendship with Ned is wrong."

I begin to panic because I don't know how else to show Tobore that Ned means nothing to me, that he, Tobore, is the one I like.

"Think this thing and tell the story to anyone you wish to. Narrate it how it is, and give me feedback, Zimife. Tell someone that you chat with a friend on Snapchat, send him pregnancy belly pictures, respond to his sexy mama comments with emojis and that his last message to you was a deal. Fucking tell someone so we see the story from a neutral perspective."

Tears fall onto my dress. Tobore stands by the door, shaking his head.

"There's a lot of strange things that have happened in whatever this is between us. From you accepting my Valentine's proposal at the last minute. I felt like a backup option to someone else that day, to asking you out because I thought I saw the signs, and you acted surprised that I asked you. You literally said you did not know. To getting pregnant and ghosting me, ghosting me during the pregnancy, calling me when you felt you were better, telling me you felt something for me out of the blue, and then this, looking for a quick comfort while I tried to shield you from what I was going through."

"What?" What did he mean by *seeking a quick comfort*?

"You embraced Ned because you needed comfort at that moment, but I cannot unsee those messages, Zim. I cannot."

I am only able to stare at him. I have no words with which to defend myself.

"We should just focus on having this child."

I search his eyes after he says this, trying to see tenderness, like always, but all I see is a darkness I have never experienced before. In the past, whenever Tobore was angry with me, his gaze would soften after a minute. Not now. The thought hits me like cold water in the face: Tobore may never again call me Sissy.

Tobore receives a call. It is the driver saying he is outside.

Without a word, I stand to leave, my knees jerking with every step.

16

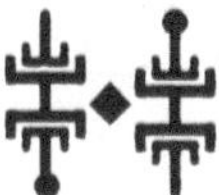

In the days that follow, I go over everything in my mind. Over and over, reading the messages between Ned and I, and thinking again about the random calls and texts we exchanged, especially the ones in the middle of the night. They all lead me back to that evening in February and I feel worse. The memory of that evening should have been a good enough reason to have never let Ned get so close to me.

I begin to ignore Belema's calls and messages. I block Ned everywhere. I keep to myself in my room. Sobenne asks and asks what troubles me until she gets tired and lets me be. The contractions come more often as the doctor predicted. At my next visit, which Sobenne had to drive me to, Dr Isioma said that my cervix had begun to efface and dilate. I did not hear the breakdown of the medical terms. Sobenne and Nelson listen. My mind drifts to Belema. How can I ever face her again, how I can tell her to her face that I fucked up. That I messed up big time.

I cry into a pillow at night so that Sobenne does not hear me. Daddy and mummy check up on me often and I pretend that what has me in this mood is the fear of labour.

"Well, I did it," Mummy says. "The women who came before me did it. Nothing will stop you from doing it. I don't have two heads. Neither did my mother nor my grandmother. We all pushed out our babies smoothly. You have absolutely nothing to fear."

Daddy is on my left rubbing my back. It is one of those days where the contractions come. But I have been told the signs of labour contractions to know when the baby is actually coming.

"Ndo, nnem," Daddy says. "It will be over soon."

Belema arrives at our house unannounced on a Saturday afternoon in early November. Perhaps she had announced it on my WhatsApp. I tossed my phone aside days ago and refused to charge it.

She walks into my room eating a banana, which Mummy must have given her. Her red dress compliments her bob wine braids and her septum-piercing glints. I wonder if Mummy complained about that piercing. Her boobs are pushed up so that her cleavage is softly revealed. She looks beautiful, as always.

"Best in Ghosting. Little Miss Ghost Mode," Belema says as she walks in, glaring at me.

I am startled and have to quickly repress an impulse to ask who let her into the house.

I have been in the room since morning, having contractions again. I have not monitored the interval between and duration of each contraction like Dr Isioma asked. At this point, I just want the baby to be on the way. I am so gravid that even my cheeks are swollen.

"Fuck. See as your belle don big," Belema says as she sits beside me.

I look up at her and suddenly break down in tears, my shoulders shaking, my back aching.

Belema makes no move to comfort me. She does not reach out to hold me or offer her shoulder for me to cry on.

"What happened, Petite? Why did you ghost again? I hope you have a better excuse this time."

A part of me wants to keep this a secret so that I can still have her, so that I do not lose out entirely during this period. Belema is one of the best things in my life. I know I messed up, but I want to hope that she might see things differently from Tobore, that she might see that this friendship with Ned was harmless.

"Belema," I croak. I avert her gaze, instead staring at my business logo. My hands are sweaty, so I rub them against the bedsheet. I feel her eyes on my hand. I wonder what it would be like to feel her rage.

"In February," I begin. "When you travelled and Ned was planning a welcome party for you, I went to his house to help him."

I find myself talking without crying anymore. I tell Belema everything that happened up till Tobore finding out. But I make no effort to bring my dead phone, to plug it into the electricity so I can show her evidence because I am abashed. I feel lighter.

Belema is silent for a while, her expression blank, and her gaze is not as fierce as it had been. It is calm. Confused, maybe, but guarded.

"I'm sorry," I say, bowing my head in shame. "I never kissed him, I swear. I never did anything with him. And the friendship for the past weeks had been nothing beyond friendship. Only friendship."

"But you allowed him to form an emotional attachment to you," she says in a tone so cold and calm. "You allowed him to be a fictional Tobore, while you waited for Tobore to come around."

"What? No. Never. He is your boyfriend and I acknowledge that."

"I complained about communication, Zimife. And you had that with him."

I have never seen Belema react to something in this way. I have never seen her so calm, without her crazy exclamations, her dramatic facial expressions or her ramblings. This Belema terrifies me.

"Cheating starts from talking, from forming an emotional bond with someone else. Ned broke up with me days ago. I called to gist about it but you refused to pick up. He broke up because he felt that we had nothing left to save; because we didn't have that spark anymore and our conversations had become boring. But I know he has been chatting with someone else online, so interested in snaps from a number saved with a love and light emoji. I guess we don't have to stalk his socials together to find out who that is."

I did not know that Ned had broken up with her. But then again, what do I know? I have ghosted everyone again. I also do not know how Ned saved my number, even though I had saved his number simply as Ned.

Belema's revelation makes me want to fall at her feet, begging and wailing until she sees just how sorry I am.

"Belema, please..." I want to cry on her lap, while she pats my head and tells me everything will be alright. I want us to name the baby together, to plan for his or her future, to hold hands while we return to UNIBEN after the strike, to save this friendship no matter what.

Belema is quiet. We are still, the silence heavy, my back aching.

"I dey tell you from time to time say you go still lose person because of this your character. I no know say na me." She lets out a short laugh. "You carry this your selfishness reach my side, Zimife. Me." She shakes her head.

I am mute as she stands up, and walks out of my room, her slippers making slap-slap sounds that grow farther away until I hear nothing. This sound will always remind me of Belema walking out of my life.

I close my eyes and tears cascade down my face.

I slide onto the floor and sob. I cry until my body is too tired and my nose gets blocked. I feel empty by the loss of the two people who had held me up in the past months. Two people who were there for me, who came back over and over again, even after everything. They did not deserve what happened and my selfish nonchalance had put us all in this terrible situation. But I do not feel like I pleaded enough. Maybe I should have grovelled, because I hurt them. But now, I have lost them. And even though Tobore might come around, I am not certain Belema ever will. Nothing is tying her to me, so that our paths might cross again.

Sobenne comes upstairs and sees me like that. She wants to know what is wrong with me, but I do not answer her, and then she snaps at me.

"This is not the time for you to be keeping things to yourself and we would be pampering you. This is a delicate time for you. What's the problem? Why are you crying like this?" She says sternly.

God forbid that Sobenne too gets so angry she does not care for me anymore. Then I would know that it is surely over for me. I open up to Sobe about the events that put me in this state.

I need to prove to Tobore and Belema that they matter to me and that despite what happened, I genuinely bore no ill intention. I imagine how hurt they both must be. I have to make an effort to let them know that I will be waiting for them. They can take as much time as they need to heal, but I will be here, waiting for them.

I charge my phone at night and send out messages to Tobore and Belema. This is not the time to be a ghost. I have to let them know just how much they mean to me, and how much I know that I messed up. And how badly I am willing to be a better person. For the next few days, every time my phone beeps, I hope it is either of them sending a response.

17

I am in the kitchen frying plantain when my water breaks. I feel a wetness along my legs and when I check, my underwear is filled with a scarlet discharge. But it is a few days before my expected date, and I crave the plantain badly, so I continue frying. I imagine I will need strength for what is coming, so I might as well eat now. I do not know how long I stay there, frying and eating, but I get carried away by my need not to panic that I do not alert anyone until an hour later, after the first contraction. It is a Tuesday and I am alone at home.

Fuck the baby is coming is what I type in the family WhatsApp group because I do not have airtime. I try to call Tobore on WhatsApp but he does not answer. He is not online. I send him a message, then I try to get the stupid airtime but my bank app is not connecting. I begin to cry as I stand there in the kitchen, an empty plate on the counter, my tights wet and bloodied, contractions gripping me intermittently.

"God, please," I say to myself. "God, please."

My hand is shaky as I order an Uber. The ride is ten minutes away. I make my way outside. The contractions last for about forty seconds long. I remember Dr Isioma said true labour contractions last between thirty and seventy seconds long. They come less than twenty-five minutes apart now, so I am trying very hard not to panic.

"God, please," I mutter again, gripping the wall until a contraction passes. I am crying because I am petrified.

The Uber arrives and the driver panics when he sees me. His scruffy beard makes his widened eyes more dramatic.

"Madam, ah! You are in labour and we dey go VI. Omo!"

Traffic is smooth until we arrive at Novare Mall. The traffic here stretches to Ogidan, threatening to trail towards Ajah. We stay in traffic for over two hours. I am restless. The contractions are fifteen to twenty minutes apart now giving me little time to catch my breath. I try to hold something, anything: the door, the chair, the headrest. I raise my legs, I close them together, and then I keep them apart. I try to kneel, try to stretch, try to squat.

Dr Isioma tells me over the phone that this is a latent phase and that I will surely be at the hospital before the active phase commences. I hope Lagos traffic allows this to happen, because if this phase is as excruciating as this, how would the next phase be? The driver keeps looking at me through the rearview mirror and sometimes turning around, telling me, "Sorry madam, sorry".

"God, please," I continue to beg, my eyes shut, my head shaking. My phone rings, I swipe to respond, but the call ends. It is Nelson.

He calls again.

"Where are you?"

"Uber... Uber o! The traffic... Nelson, the traffic," I scream. I am crying even more now, my sobs are so loud that I see hawkers looking into the car, staring at me with pity. Nelson is saying something but I cannot hear him. My heart is pounding so loudly the sounds fill my ears.

"Jesus," I gasp, changing my position again.

"Sorry, madam," the driver says again. He drives frantically.

After we escape the traffic at Ogidan, we dive into the one at VGC.

I almost alight from the Uber to walk forward while the traffic lessens, but Nelson calls me at this time.

"Stay in the car, Zimife!" He yells.

"Why are you shouting at me?" I cry. "If you think this is easy then come and do it."

Dr Isioma speaks into the phone. "Calm down, Zim. Try to take deep breaths, deep breaths." I do as she says, inhaling and exhaling with so much force so I can fucking feel better.

I can hear Nelson's distant voice. He sounds agitated, snapping at how congested Lagos is and how this traffic is pissing him off.

Nelson and Dr Isioma stay on the phone with me while I cry. My back aches so much that sitting down is torture. My legs feel so heavy, my stomach feels lower than it was, as if the baby is sliding down already.

"Jesus!"

"Driver, where una dey?" Nelson asks.

The driver turns around and speaks in the direction of my phone.

"We don reach Chevron now."

"Una don dey reach. Abeg, take care of am. Abeg. Na my sister."

I scream again, scratching the car doors.

"Sorry, madam. Easy."

When we arrive at the hospital, the pain has become unbearable. My legs tremble and my tears would not stop. The smell of disinfectant assaults my nose and makes me feel worse. I groan. Dr Isioma runs pelvic exams to determine the dilation of the cervix.

"She's active," she says to the nurses around me. "She's five centimetres dilated."

Nelson rushes to my side after I have changed into a hospital gown and have been asked to walk up and down as the contractions increase.

I take his hand in mine and squeeze it as a contraction runs its course. He winces.

I am pacing and, when I turn around, I see Mummy and Daddy standing at the reception. Daddy is praying, Mummy looks much calmer, but her eyes are fiery. I exhale with my mouth. Nelson rubs my back and holds my right hand. Outside, I see the sun setting in the sky. Birds fly across amber clouds. What if I do not see another day? What if I die with this pain?

I turn away from the window and cry harder. What if this baby does not make it? My cries become louder. I close my eyes and begin to mutter prayers. I call out to the Virgin Mary. I recall Mummy's words. She did not have two heads, neither did Mama and neither did the Virgin Mary who birthed Jesus.

"Hail Mary full of grace," I begin. Nelson is still holding my hand. And so, he joins in my muttering. "The Lord is with thee. Blessed are you amongst women, and blessed is the fruit of thy womb, Jesus."

Mummy comes close to me, and Nelson steps aside. She presses her oily index finger to my forehead, her fingers making the sign of the cross.

"This birth shall be smooth. This journey shall end in praise. You did not carry this child for nine whole months to lose it. You did not carry this child for nine months to lose yourself, nwam. You will see that the God we serve does incredible things. He has never failed us, and he will not start now." "Amen," I say.

"Ngwa, Jigidem. Hold your sister," she commands, moving away with her eyes closed, her lips moving.

As Nelson comes close to me, I catch, at the entrance door, looking left and right, Tobore, as if looking for something he had lost. A contraction grips me just then and I scream.

I am wheeled into the delivery room on a stretcher, my body glistering with sweat. Dr Isioma, two nurses and Mummy are with me. Mummy is wearing a nose mask, hospital gown and gloves. My eyes shut briefly just as we arrive. The room smells of antiseptic, Dr Isioma and the nurses set me to sit up, connect tubes to my wrists, wash my lower back with cold antiseptic and give me an epidural shot.

The pain subsides shortly after and my body slumps against the bed, relieved.

When they shout, "Push," I feel so lightheaded and lethargic. All I want to do is succumb to the weightlessness. Maybe if I just close my eyes a bit. The noise around me and the beeping monitors begin to fade out. I just want to sleep.

Light taps on my cheek causes my eyes to open lazily. Staring above me is Mummy. She is saying something. She seems agitated. A nurse gently nudges her away and taps my cheek continually and then, as if being pulled out of a trance, I jerk awake. The nurses, Dr Isioma, and Tobore, all surround me. Tobore takes my hand in his.

"You can do this," he says.

I nod, gripping his hand and squeezing the sheets with my other hand. I grunt loudly.

"Push!" I hear. I push.

I continue pushing until I feel a widening in my centre. I push again and I feel a weight slide out of me and a tiny shriek in the air.

My body collapses on the bed. I feel something else slide out of me. I feel a painful relief as I heave. Tobore is holding my hand and laughing, looking down at me.

I want to see my baby. I want to hold my baby. My eyes dart around. I remove my hand from Tobore's. I see the nurse holding up my baby and I stretch my hands out to receive the small body. After everything that I have been through today, that the baby has been through today, we deserve to hold on to each other.

"It's a girl," the nurse says as she hands me the tiny form with blood smears on her greasy, creamy body. I stare at the wailing child and my body shakes with giddiness. I did this. I gave birth to this tiny human. I did this. I have a baby. I have a child. This one is mine. I want to be a mother to her. I want to be a good mother.

As I hold my baby against my skin, Tobore rubs my shoulder. He looks thrilled. I do not know what life will be like beyond this room. All I know is that I am here. In spite of all the people who show up standing outside the delivery room, who pace in the lobby, who pray to God, who held my hand, who have waited for my child to be born, I still feel the void. Tobore is here only as a father, not as a friend nor lover. Belema is nowhere.

"Do you have a name in mind, Zim?" Tobore asks, a small smile on his face. He does not call me Sissy.

Ashamed, I shake my head.

"No, not yet."

Tobore sighs, his eyes on our daughter. "Isio, because she is a star."

"I like that." I smile, looking up at him. "I really like that."

"Me too." His smile is soft. He is here only for the baby as I am sure he always will.

He may forgive me with time. But we may never have what we had. And I know that this is my punishment, so I must endure this pain.

I keep looking at the door to see if Belema would walk through, if she would show her face and just say something funny. I am tired. I want to close my eyes and rest. Although, I am happy to have had a successful birth, my joy is not full. Belema is not here.

Later, when Isio is cleaned up and I have been moved to the ward, after my family troops in one by one to see the baby, their voices loud, their eyes proud and smiling, I lie alone, waiting. My gaze keeps wandering to the door. Maybe she will lean against the doorframe, her eyes on me, having waited for everyone to leave so that she can have her moment. And maybe when my eyes meet hers, she would stand straighter, her eyes brighter as she smiles at me. I smile in return, signalling her to come over. She comes over, slaps my forearm lightly and screams.

"You did it, Petite. You born pikin!"

And then we would laugh, our voices echoing down the hallway, our bodies shaking from giddiness. She would give Isio a name, and then a nickname and we would stick to it.

My smile wanes, my eyes water and everything is a blur.

Tobore walked out of the delivery room earlier and I have not seen him since then. Has he too left me already?

Sobenne walks in. I do not see her until she is near me, shaking my shoulder. She is in her work clothes—a beige chiffon blouse and a pleated black skirt that hugs her hips. The low pumps I saw her leave with in the morning has been replaced with ugly rubber slippers. I suspect she bought it in traffic.

"Hey."

I look up at her, my eyes wide, trying to keep the tears from brimming to my eyes.

"Hey," I say, forcing a smile.

She stares at me for a while, her eyes searching mine. She rubs my shoulder lightly, and hands me a card. I frown as I collect it from her. It is a congratulatory card.

Sobenne's pity does not care to hide itself.

She clears her throat.

"Tobore went to get you pepper soup."

"Oh," I say. A small smile appears on my lips. He will be back. Then she nods at the card.

"Belema stopped by. She brought some gifts and asked me to give you that. Said she had to rush back." I open the card.

Dear Zimi, be a good mother to your daughter, a good sister and a good daughter. Congratulations on your delivery, I wish you the very best. Take care.

I read the letter over and over again, my eyes running through the lines, seeking more. Take care—a kind of "Goodbye, have a fun life, see you never."

Dear? Dear Zimi? There would be no Petite anymore.

I stare at the card long enough for a tear to fall. I fucked up.

Sobenne is still by my side. She does not rub my back, or hold me close. She just stands and watches me. And for the first time,

I like this privacy. I want to cry on my own. I do not need to be consoled. I want to drown in this feeling. I dug this hole myself.

Sobenne sits beside me, her gaze on the baby's cot, which is not so far from my bed.

"You just need to give them time to heal before you go chasing them."

I stare at her. "I don't know."

"You don't want to chase after them?"

I shake my head quickly. "I do. I do, so much."

Sobenne smiles. "Good. Because when you love someone, you must stop at nothing to show it to them. You messed up, and they need to know that you know you messed up. Forgiveness begins from there. You hear me, Baby?"

"Yes, loud and clear," I say and laugh, wiping my tears.

"Good. Because after you have rested well, you will find the people you love and express to them just how much you love them. You will ask for their forgiveness, and before them, you will acknowledge your mistake. Only then can they forgive you, and can you also forgive yourself."

I embrace Sobenne tightly. "Thank you," I whisper against her ears. She rubs my back, holding me as tightly. When she lets go, she kisses my cheek, stands up from the bed and leaves the room.

Nelson walks in after Sobenne leaves. His large body makes the room seem smaller. It is the second time he has come to see the baby. He is in his lab coat this time, and his name is sewn into the right breast area. *Pharm. N. Ike-Steven.* He cocks his head to the side.

"You are not asleep? Isioma says you need to rest."

I laugh and shake my head. Then I sit up gently. I look from the baby to him, and I recall all that happened from nine months ago up until today. I do not think I regret wanting to rid myself of the baby months ago, because maybe if I had succeeded, many of the things that have happened could have been avoided. But I also do not fault the baby for everything that happened. It was all on me. And the baby deserves to live a life free of guilt. That is my burden to bear, and I would not have her experience any of it.

I think I owe Nelson some gratitude. He did something that we never spoke of, and I never showed just how grateful I was for that.

I pat the side of the bed and gesture for him to come over.

He stares at me, unsure. Then he walks over and sits beside me, still gazing at the baby cot, a small smile on his face.

"Thank you," I say, my eyes on my hands. "For not telling anyone I planned to abort the baby."

He shakes his head. "They would have been disappointed. It would have broken Daddy's heart so much. They were already really disappointed, you know? And they were for a long time."

I laugh. "It would have lasted longer if Tobore and I did not sort of get together, and maybe that's okay. This is not what they expected of me at this point in my life. But it has happened and we cannot turn back the hands of time."

Nelson faces me, surprised, and then he smiles and nods.

"Well, look who has suddenly grown up."

I guffaw and immediately regret it because my vagina aches as I do.

Nelson sighs.

"They could never have stayed angry with you forever. They love you, Zimi. You made a mistake. But they gave you shelter, checked up on you, and when the whole prenatal stuff was eating deep into my salary, they came in. They began making plans." He turns to me.

"With or without Tobore, they would have loved you; they would still have embraced you. Although Tobore made that process faster, it would still have happened."

My eyes well up with tears. "But mummy was always so angry," I whisper, my voice shaky. "She would comment every time she passed beside me. Daddy was so cold to me. Only when Tobore and I began to look serious did they look at my side. And I wonder what would happen now that Tobore and I are not even together.

We never really were anyway."

Nelson stares at me, his eyes clear. "You should just talk to them. Say your mind, so that their behaviour does not depress you. Tell them how you feel and how you have felt in the past months. They will understand. And if they don't, you have to make peace with the fact that you tried. Then just look ahead. Your whole life is still ahead of you."

I stare long at Nelson, allowing my tears to fall from the corner of my eyes. My nose gets blocked, and as I wheeze, my vagina aches.

Nelson stands up from the bed and shoves his hand into his pocket.

"I should get going. I have work."

"Help me call them in, please."

"No," he says promptly. "You will talk to them later, please. Isioma will not be happy to see people trooping in and out of the room when you should be resting."

I press my lips in a thin line. "But you disobeyed her."

He glares at me. "I am also a medical practitioner." "Wonderful." I wriggle my brows.

His glare dissolves and he laughs softly.

"You better be going before my doctor catches you here, Pharm."

He gazes at me tenderly and smiles. "Rest, Zimi. Get some sleep. You will see them later, alright?"

I nod. "Thank you."

He smiles as he walks out.

With Nelson gone, my eyes are still wide open, staring at the cot where my baby sleeps. I will speak my truth when my parents come. I will clear the assumption that Tobore and I are together. They need to understand that I am aware that I made a mistake, but what else can I do other than shape my life to be better from here onwards and be the best person that I can be? I will express myself irrespective of what happens from here because I need to start facing these things head-on. When I am discharged from the hospital, I will find Tobore and Belema and tell them how truly sorry I am.

The door creaks and I turn absently towards it, turn back to the cot reflexively and then immediately turn back to the door as it opens fully. I am stunned, my heart on the verge of bursting.

Belema stands there in a batik blouse and a pair of black faded jeans, and when her gaze meets mine, I blink rapidly and swallow. I sniff to keep my tears from falling. She walks quietly towards the baby's cot.

But for the light squeaks of the ceiling fan, nothing else makes a sound.

"She'll look like you, Petite. I don dey see her nose," Belema says. My heart races. I burst into tears while laughing. My vagina aches but I continue anyway.

"Nke iru ka," I whisper, staring at the cot. And then I say it louder, as though realising what it truly means. Belema turns to stare at me, eyebrow raised.

"Iruka," I say again, my eyes darting to the baby.

Belema walks over to the bed and sits by my feet. She looks at me and nods.

"I like it."

End

Acknowledgement

This, shockingly, is the hardest part of writing a story. There is a long list of people to thank, but I'll keep it brief.

First, I give thanks to God—I prayed and dreamt of this, and He brought it to life.

To my parents, Engr. Eric Chijioke and Mrs. Esther Chijioke—when I picked up a pen to write, sometime in 2013, you both flipped through the pages with eagerness. In the years since then, you have nudged me on, asked about my new writings, read all my books, and encouraged me. To say that I am blessed to have you both does not suffice. Thank you for being my numero unos.

Kamsi, Kaosulu, and Neto—brothers who read simply because their sister writes, whose eyes sparkle with pride and whose shoulders lift because their sister is achieving her dreams as a writer.

Mrs. Gbemi Shasore—thank you for creating opportunities for dreamers like me. It is because of initiatives like yours that I continue to let my creative flowers bloom. To my editor, Nurain Ali-Balogun—thank you for your prompt responses, the countless emails, and for seeing this story the way I do. Working with you has been a pleasure. To Teniola Akinwalere, for your support in this entire process, thank you.

To the judges of Quramo Writers Prize 2023—Lechi Eke, Anote Ajeluorou and Dr Eghosa Imasuen—thank you for being wowed by this story and for seeing it in a way that I never did— a winning story. To the entire team of Quramo Publishing and Quramo Writers' Prize, thank you for deeming this story worthy, and for giving writers an opportunity to believe in something so great. Thank you.

Andrea Hare—for the crying emojis, constructive reviews, detailed feedback, and the great belief that this is the story— thank you. You've been both the writer's reader and the writer's writer. Toluwaleyi Keshinro, Pelumi Obisan and Tsemaye Solo-Edema, thank you for agreeing to be beta readers of this story's early drafts. Because you believed in it, I did too.

To Osian Sophia, for being so eager to hold my book in hardcover, for your fervent prayers and love, thank you. To Efobi Lotanna—thank you for listening to me endlessly talk about this story, for being the medical adviser and for being so proudly in my corner.

To my family—the Enemos and the Aniebosis—friends and well-wishers, thank you for seeing me in a light so bright, and for mentioning my name beside literary greats. It showed how profound your faith in me was and still is. I love you all and I look forward to prouder moments.

9 783901 176777